Freehand Pattern Drawing

Freehand Pattern Drawing

32 antique designs to challenge and improve
your artistic skills

by EA Branch

JM
CLASSIC EDITIONS

This edition digitally re-mastered and
published by JM Classic Editions © 2007
Original text © EA Branch 1905

ISBN 978-1-905217-91-5

CONTENTS.

———◆———

AUTHOR'S NOTE.

THIS book should prove to be not only a complete course of *Freehand Drawing in Outline*, but also very useful to students of *Elementary Principles of Ornament* and *Elementary Design*. One feature which the Author believes to be quite new in a book on Freehand Drawing, is the Summary of the *Principles of Ornament* and *Construction of Pattern*.

The examples have been selected with great care from the South Kensington Museum, to present to the student as complete an idea as possible of the treatment of ornament in different materials. *Inlays, patterns on pottery, textiles, wrought-iron, repoussé, carved work in wood* and *stone*, &c., are all represented. Examples of *Natural foliage* are also added.

Each example is thoroughly analysed and a complete set of working diagrams given. Treatment with either pen or brush is illustrated in every case, in order that the interpretation of ornament with either medium may be thoroughly understood.

The student is also shown clearly how to deal with difficulties arising from *accidents* due either to the limitations of the material, the process of manufacture, unequal stretching in the case of fabrics, and wear and tear, &c., in others.

Students preparing for the King's Scholarship or the South Kensington Examinations should find this specially adapted to their requirements.

The Author desires to cordially thank the Authorities at South Kensington Museum for their kindness and courtesy in allowing the reproduction of the Plates.

E. A. B., *1905*.

INTRODUCTION.

SUGGESTIONS AS TO STUDY.

EVERY copy should be proceeded with in the order of the following steps :—

Setting-Out.—The most important principle to be observed when commencing to set-out a copy is that of Proportion. First, the relation of the width to the height must be ascertained very carefully, and set out in pencil on the paper.

Next, the chief divisions must be set-out before an attempt is made to draw any line of the ornament itself. The position of certain distinguishing forms should be noted, such as the edge of a scroll, centre of a rosette, base or top of a flower-form, &c. The Student should ascertain whether they occur, say, half-way across the copy, a third, or a fourth, and so on. Diagram 1 on each plate shows how in each copy the important divisions have first been found and then set-out.

Leading Lines.—These are the structure lines upon which the whole ornament is based. They should be drawn as the next step after the setting out of the various proportions and positions of the chief parts. They are also shown in each case in Diagram 1.

Leading Lines play the same part in ornament as the skeleton does in the animal body and stems do in plants. No copy should be proceeded with until a complete skeleton of leading lines is obtained.

Blocking-Out.—If the photo be observed with half-closed eyes, the shapes of the masses and the spaces between can be readily seen. The general shape of these masses, both large and small, should be drawn until the drawing appears in every case like Diagram 2. At this stage use as many straight lines as possible to indicate the general outline of the masses.

Forms.—After the blocking-out is done, the next step is to put into each block the *shapes* of the various forms composing the ornament, such as leaves, flowers, &c., as the case may be.

Details.—Lastly, the details are to be added. This ought not to be difficult if the blocks have been made the right size and shape and in their correct positions, and if the leaf, fruit and flower forms have been filled into them carefully. Diagram 3 on each plate shows very clearly how the details are to be rendered. They consist chiefly of serrations, veins and pipes in leaves, petals in flowers, and features in animal and fish forms.

At the South Kensington and Scholarship Examinations the drawings may be finished either with pencil, pen or brush. To finish with the pen use a nib of medium softness. Avoid a hard one, as it gives harsh wiry lines. To line in **PEN AND BRUSH WORK.** with the brush use a No. 2 or 3 sable water colour brush and very dilute ink, so as to obtain a soft *grey* line. When making a stroke with the brush, draw the fingers in towards the palm of the hand; this ensures a smooth steady stroke. Washing-in a background requires a great deal of practice in order to avoid a patchy appearance. It must be done with a full brush, charged with very dilute black ink, in the same way that colour is put upon a map.

Some patterns can be expressed in "silhouette" with the brush, that is, the colour is washed into the forms exactly up to the pencil lines, and when dry the drawing is cleaned up, leaving the forms without any outline round them. (*See* Plates XII. and XXIV., Diagrams 3.)

INTERPRETING THE PLATES.

No accidents are to be copied, such as a line being carried too far or bent somewhat out of its true curvature, owing to unequal stretching of the material, to tearing, to age, or to distortion in the photographing. The *intention* of the designer is to be rendered, and not a mere servile copying of distortions in the photograph. In the case of Applique work (*see* Chair Back), the cord round the edges of all the forms is a feature of the design, and must be shown by doubling the outline. (*See* Plates VI., IX. and X., Diagram 3.) In woven textiles, carpets, &c., the edges of the curves appear sometimes to be made up of little squares, so that they have a saw-like outline. No notice whatever is to be taken of this, but the "form" is to be drawn with a smooth flowing line in the usual way. Look at such photographs for a few minutes with half-closed eyes, when the "forms" with their required curvature will gradually become evident. (*See* Plates VIII. and XVIII.)

Students' drawings should be considerably larger than the Photographs. The sheet of drawing paper should be half-imperial (22 in. by 15 in.) and the drawing should *fairly* fill it, leaving a reasonable margin all round.

All the Plates in this book, with the exceptions of Nos. XXI. and XXII. are examples of *Conventional Ornament*, that is, ornament which consists of a design based upon some flower or other form found in Nature, but not a *direct copy* of that flower or form. Plates XXI. and XXII. are photographs of natural plants, and cannot be included under the term *Ornament*.

PRINCIPLES OF ORNAMENT.

(1) **Proportion.**—This is the ratio or relation which one part of the ornament bears to the whole. Not only must the relation of height to width of the *whole copy* be found, and also that of one part to another, but in drawing all the forms, both large and small, due regard must be paid to the proportions of their own width to their length.

(2) **Radiation.**—Lines are said to radiate when they suggest common growth or origin. This principle abounds in nature. The petals of most flowers radiate from a centre; radiation is seen in the growth of leaves from a stem, feathers in a bird's wing, &c. Lines can radiate from (*a*) a centre, (*b*) a straight line, (*c*) a curved line.

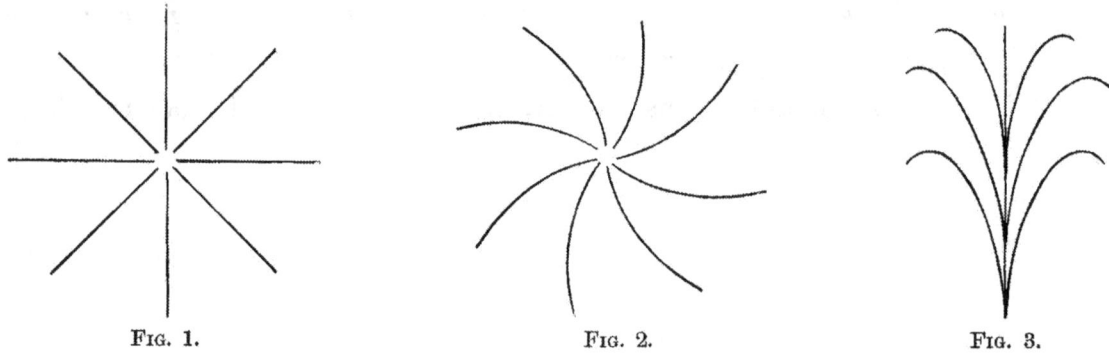

FIG. 1.　　　　FIG. 2.　　　　FIG. 3.

For lines to radiate artistically they must grow out at a tangent from the leading line and not appear as if stuck into it. A line, intended to be radiating, should not cut through the leading line when produced.

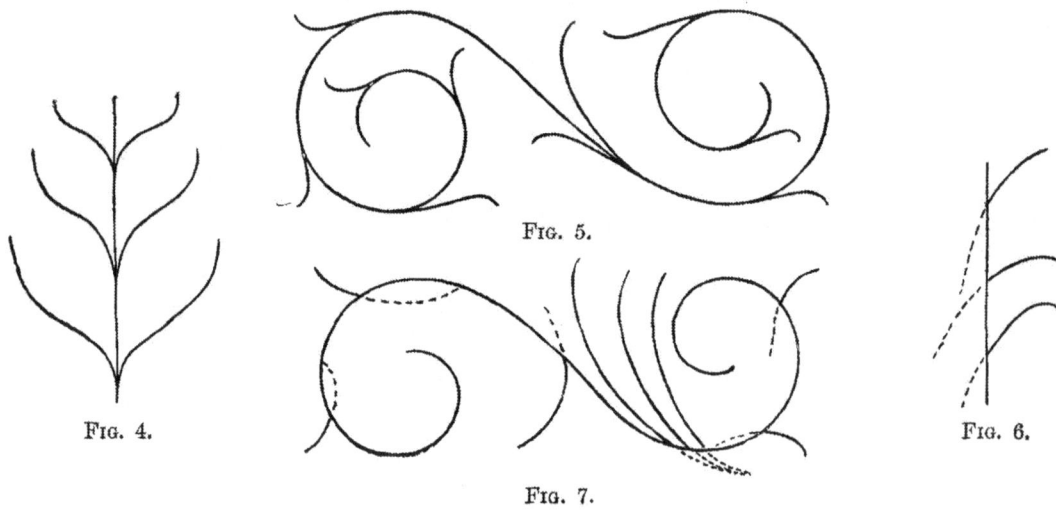

FIG. 5.

FIG. 4.　　　　FIG. 7.　　　　FIG. 6.

(3) **Tangential Junction.**—This follows from good radiation. It is the joining of lines at a tangent so that they appear to grow out of each other, as shown in Figs. 3, 4, 5.

(4) Continuity.—Frequently a leading line, a stem, or some other form passes under another form and reappears again. Its reappearance must be so drawn that the eye easily recognises it to be the continuation of the previous form. This is known as Continuity of Form. Sometimes certain forms (such as stems) spring from a source which is covered up by another part of the ornament. In all these cases the complete form must be drawn right through the part which covers it. The part not required in the finished drawing can be cleaned out.

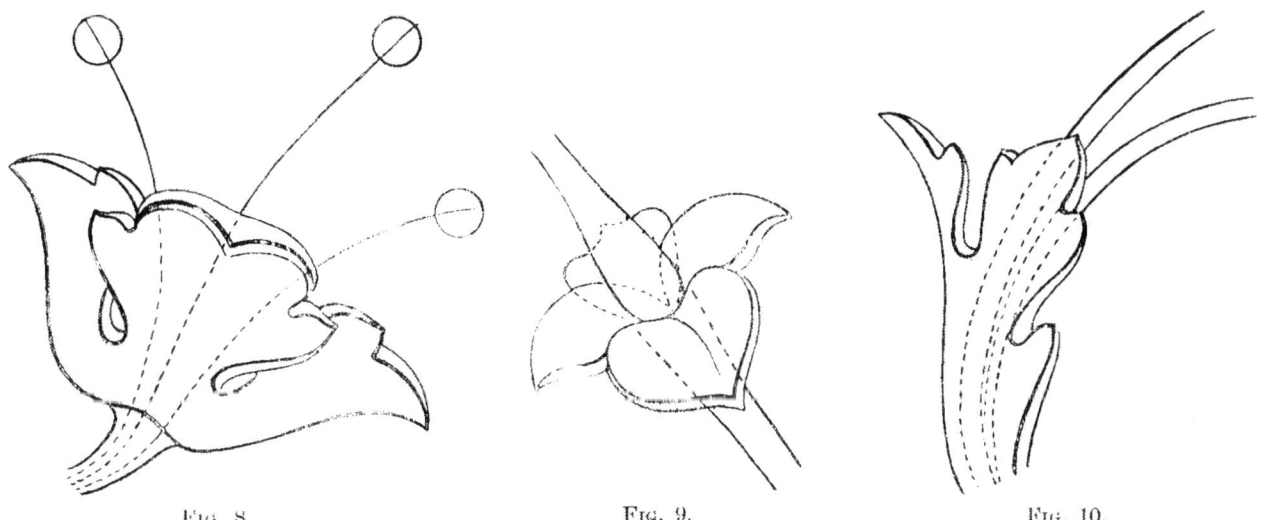

Fig. 8.　　　　Fig. 9.　　　　Fig. 10.

(5) Acanthus Forms.—These are conventional forms of the Acanthus leaf; the natural leaf somewhat resembles a vine leaf. The curves used in the drawing of the leaf are almost all exclusively "lines of beauty," thus:

To draw an Acanthus or similar leaf proceed as follows:—

    (a) Block out the general shape of the leaf.
    (b) Fix the position of the eyes.
    (c) Block out the lobes.
    (d) Draw the serrations.
    (e) Add relief (if any).

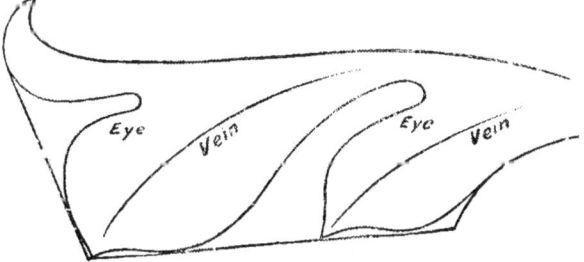

Fig. 11.—*Showing Three Lobes.*

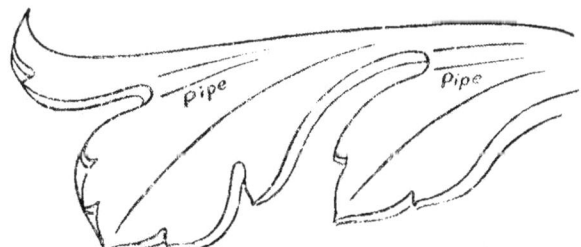

Fig. 11.—*Showing Serrations and Relief.*

(9)

For conventional forms of Acanthus foliage, *see* Plates V., VI., IX., X., XI., XVI. to XX.

(6) **Relief.**—This is the raised appearance which carved or modelled ornament has. To produce this effect in outline, those edges of the ornament which are raised up from the background are represented by a strong dark line, whilst the lower edges which are nearly or quite upon the background are represented by a somewhat lighter line. *See* Diagrams 3 in Plates XIII. to XVII.

NATURAL FOLIAGE.

Stems and Junctions.—Six photos are given of natural foliage, whose treatment is practically the same as if they were photographed from *casts*. (Plates XXI., XXII. and XXIX.—XXXII.) These sprays must be set out in the same manner as any other copy, the position of important points and divisions having been first noted, and the main stems drawn as leading lines. (*See* Diagram 1.) Next the *masses* of leaves, fruit or flowers must be blocked out, and the general shape of the separate leaves filled in, using as many straight lines as possible. (Note Diagram 2 carefully.)

The stems must be kept strong and vigorous, the sections being practically straight lines. The joining of leaves to the main stem is the commonest source of error. Avoid making the stalk of leaf appear to be stuck into the stem as at A, but notice that the joint appears to wrap itself partly round the stem, as at B.

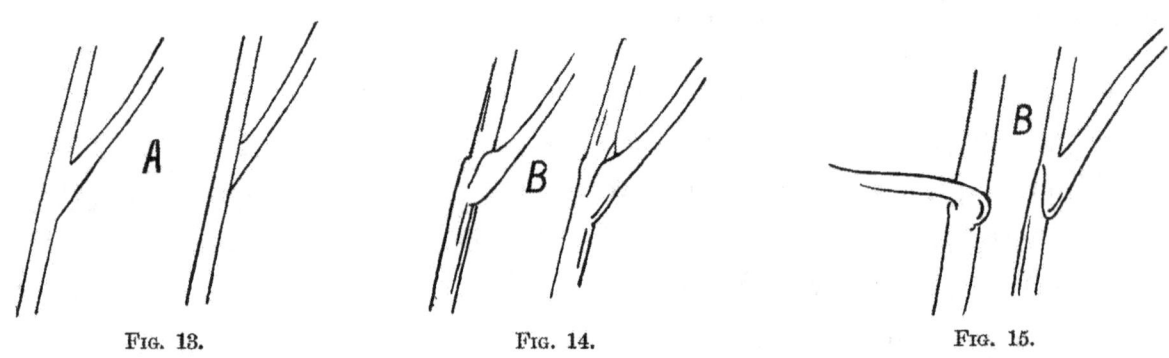

FIG. 13. FIG. 14. FIG. 15.

Veining.—The most important line in a leaf is the mid-rib or central vein, which, it will be observed, is the *continuation of the stalk itself* right along the middle of the leaf up to the tip. This is particularly noticeable at the back of a leaf. (*See* Diagrams 3, Plates XXI. and XXII.) The secondary veins and net veins are clearly shown also in the same diagrams. They must be kept much lighter and finer than the outline of the leaf itself. The nearer edge of every leaf should be made stronger than the remoter.

Rectangularity.—The balancing of a form such as a fruit or blossom upon its stalk in a plane at right angles to the direction of the stalk is known as rectangularity. To secure this, always draw the stalk right through the fruit or blossom, and then balance the latter equally on each side of it at right angles.

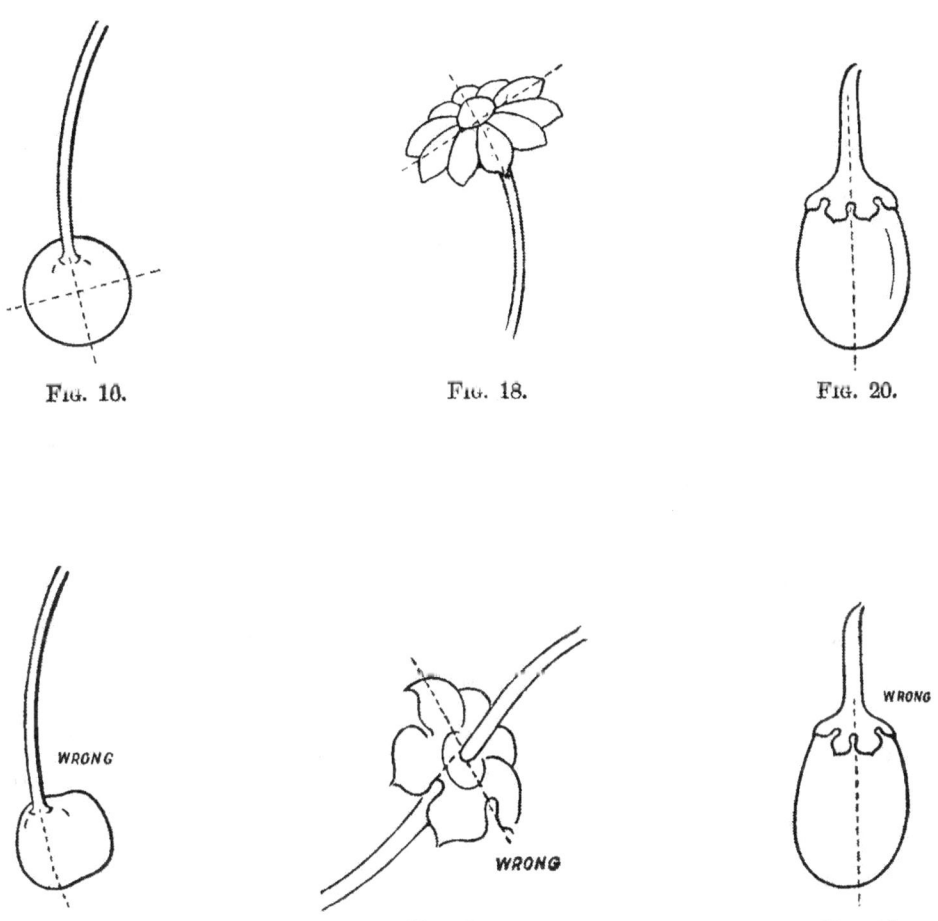

Fig. 16.

Fig. 18.

Fig. 20.

Fig. 17.

Fig. 19.

Fig. 21.

THE CONSTRUCTION OF PATTERN.

———◆———

A certain amount of knowledge of the Construction of Pattern is necessary for the drawing of repeating patterns in textiles, inlays, &c. Examples of repeating patterns, or diapers, as they are called, are to be found in wall-papers, linoleums, carpets, cretonnes, curtains, &c.

Repeating pattern consists of a *Unit of Design* repeated over and over again in at east two directions in a defined and orderly arrangement. The *Unit* generally consists of some ornamental form which fills either a square, rectangle, triangle, lozenge, or hexagon, &c. To obtain the defined and orderly arrangement a NET is used, and the *Unit of Repeat* is either filled into the meshes of the net or placed at regular intervals on the intersections of the lines forming the NET.

The lines of the net itself are used to obtain certain ornamental geometric forms, and when this is done a MOTIVE is said to be obtained. In other cases the intersections of the net are used as centres from which arcs are described forming MOTIVES of ornamental curves. (*See* diagrams below.)

Close attention is directed to the following NETS with MOTIVES upon them. They are greatly reduced, the meshes in the originals being about four or five inches wide. In making a copy of these the whole work must be done by freehand. The student should endeavour to design new motives for himself, and he will be surprised at the great variety which can be formed upon these simple nets. The nets most commonly used are the *square, rectangle, triangle* and *lattice*.

NETS AND MOTIVES.

A MOTIVE is only the skeleton upon which a design is worked. Study the diapers in Plates XXIII. to XXVIII., giving close attention to diagrams, which show the NETS and MOTIVES upon which the patterns are based, and also the manner of setting out the large masses of the design. Plate XXVII. is based upon a motive similar to that shown in Fig. 39, while Plate XXVIII. is based upon one similar to Fig. 40.

To Draw a Repeating Pattern.—

(1) Discover and draw the *Net*.

(2) Draw the *Motive* (if any).

(3) Set out the *Masses* throughout the whole pattern.

(4) Completely draw one "unit of repeat" *at least*.

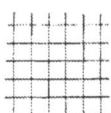

Fig. 22.
Square net.

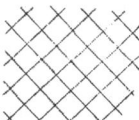

Fig. 23.
*Square net set at 45°
(diamond-wise).*

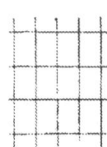

Fig. 24.
Oblong net.

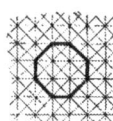

Fig. 25.
*Combined square
nets.*

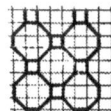

Fig. 26.
*Octagon and squares
as motives on a
square net.*

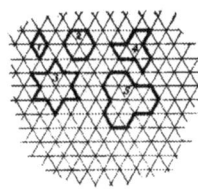

Fig. 27.
*Net composed of equilateral
triangles. Forms obtained
from combination of
triangles.*

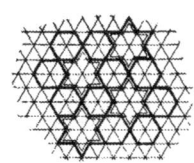

Fig. 28.
*Motive of stars and hexagons
on a triangular net.*

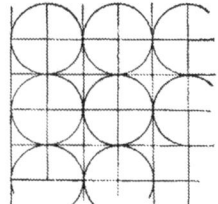

Fig. 29.
*Motive of tangential circles
on square net.*

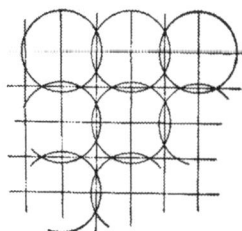

Fig. 30.
*Motive of interlacing circles
on square net.*

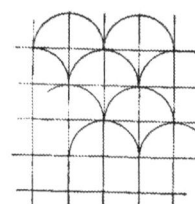

Fig. 31.
*Motive of semicircles form-
ing "imbrication" on
square net.*

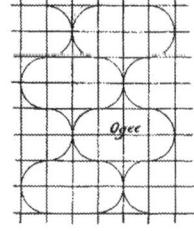

Fig. 32.
*Motive of semicircles form-
ing "ogees" on a square
net.*

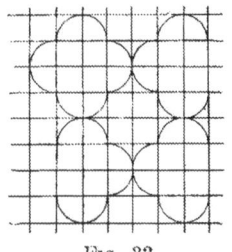

Fig. 33.
*Motive of semicircles form-
ing "quatrefoils."*

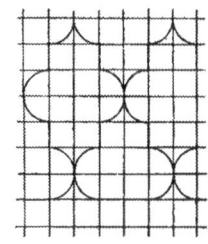

Fig. 34.
*Motive of semicircles and
lines forming "broken
ogees."*

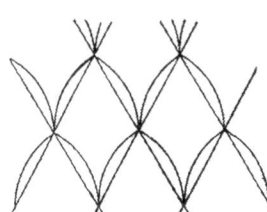

Fig. 35.
*Motive of arcs on a "lattice
net" forming "imbrication."*

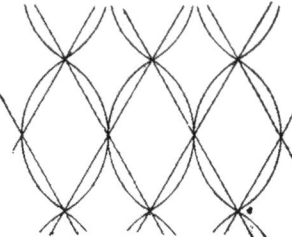

Fig. 36.
Motive of arcs on a "lattice net."

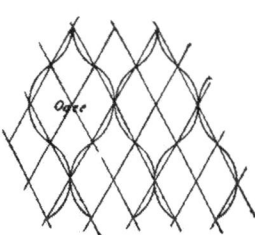

Fig. 37.
*Motive of arcs on a "lattice
net" forming "ogees."*

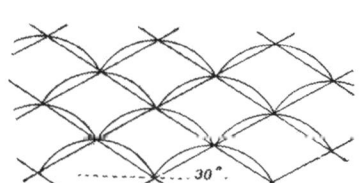

Fig. 38.
*Motive of arcs forming "imbrica-
tion" on a lattice net, the lines of
which are set at 30°.*

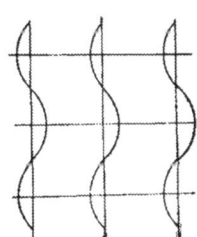

Fig. 39.
*Vertical "wave" motive on
square net.*

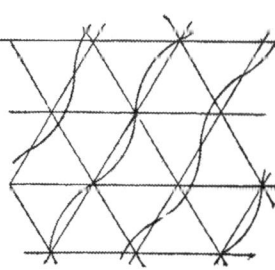

Fig. 40.
*Oblique "wave" motive on a
triangular net.*

Thirty-two

ART DESIGNS

WITH

iLLUSTRATIVE DIAGRAMS.

PLATE I.

SYRIAN TILE FROM CAIRO.

White on Blue Ground.   About 13th Century.

STAGE I.—Set out the square about 11 inches wide. Draw the diameters and diagonals. Next draw the circle to contain the octagonal form in the centre. Its proportion to the whole square must be most carefully ascertained. On comparing it will be found to be rather more than a quarter of the width of the tile. Next draw the general shape of the large masses in each quarter. Their length will be found to be one-third of the diagonals.

STAGE II.—Draw the general shape of the smaller masses, giving great attention to their relative size.

STAGE III.—Into *all* the general shapes fill in the details in pencil. After that line-in with pen or brush, and finally, if you so wish, wash in a tone of very dilute ink, as shown.

N.B.—Do not copy accidents, due to imperfect workmanship or to the manufacturing process. If a line is bent out of its true curvature or carried too far, it must not be copied so. Look at the whole design and see what was *intended*, and if one part be ill-defined, another similar portion of the pattern will indicate what should be drawn.

PLATE I.

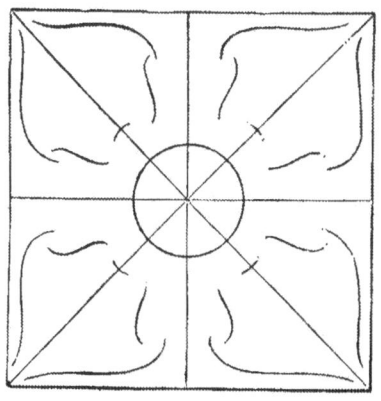

STAGE I.

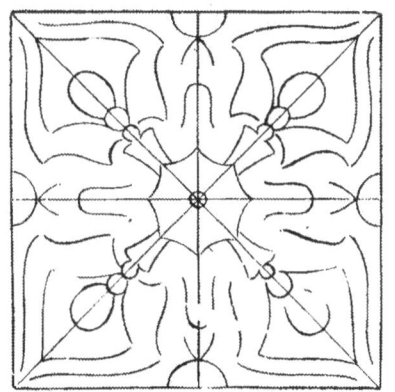

STAGE II.

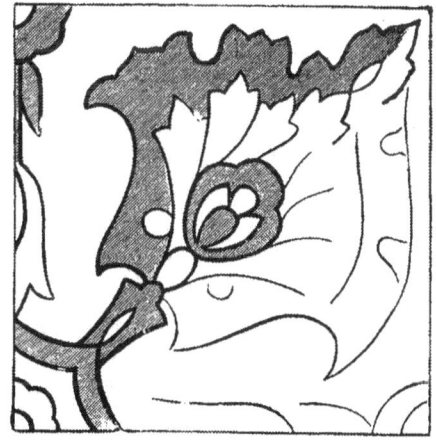

STAGE III.

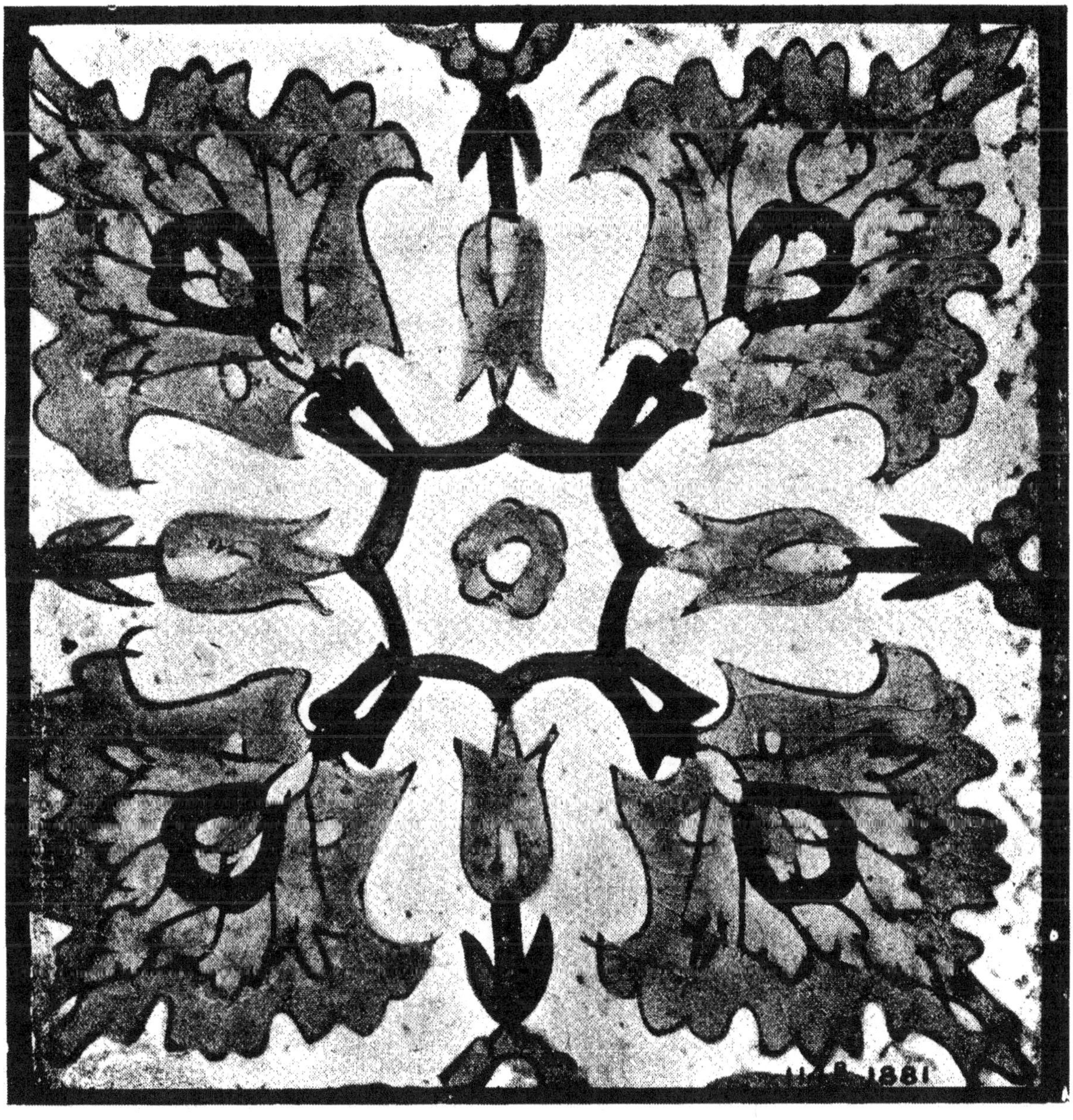

SYRIAN TILE FROM CAIRO.

By permission, South Kensington Museum.

(17)

PLATE II.

ELECTROTYPE PLATE.

The original plate is of Silver, forming a portion of the Perak Regalia. Repousse work engraved.   Malay, 18th Century.

STAGE I.—Set out the circle about 11 inches wide. The eight diameters should then be drawn, and the other circles in proportion to each other. The leading lines of the curves radiating from the centre should next be put in, each balanced upon a diameter.

STAGE II.—Draw all the forms in the central design. A small piece of the running pattern round the edge of the plate need only be drawn, but it should be done carefully.

N.B.—The edges of the central design must be drawn quite smoothly, of perfect curvature, as shown in Diagram 2, though in the original they are not so. This is due to the limitations of the material and method of work. The design is beaten up from the back with a hammer, hence the lack of a sharp and clearly defined edge to the forms. This is characteristic of repousse work.

PLATE II.

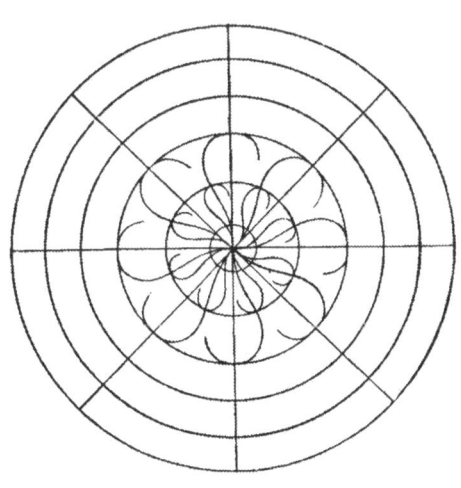

STAGE I.

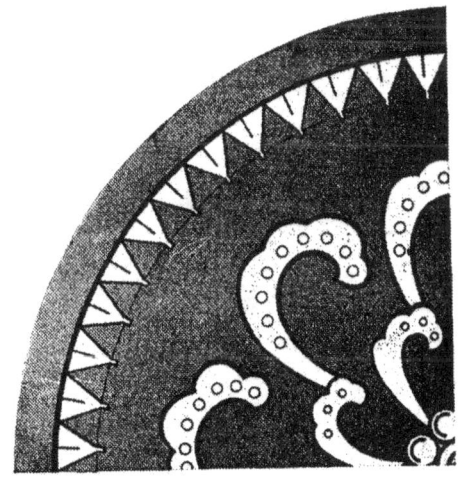

STAGE II.

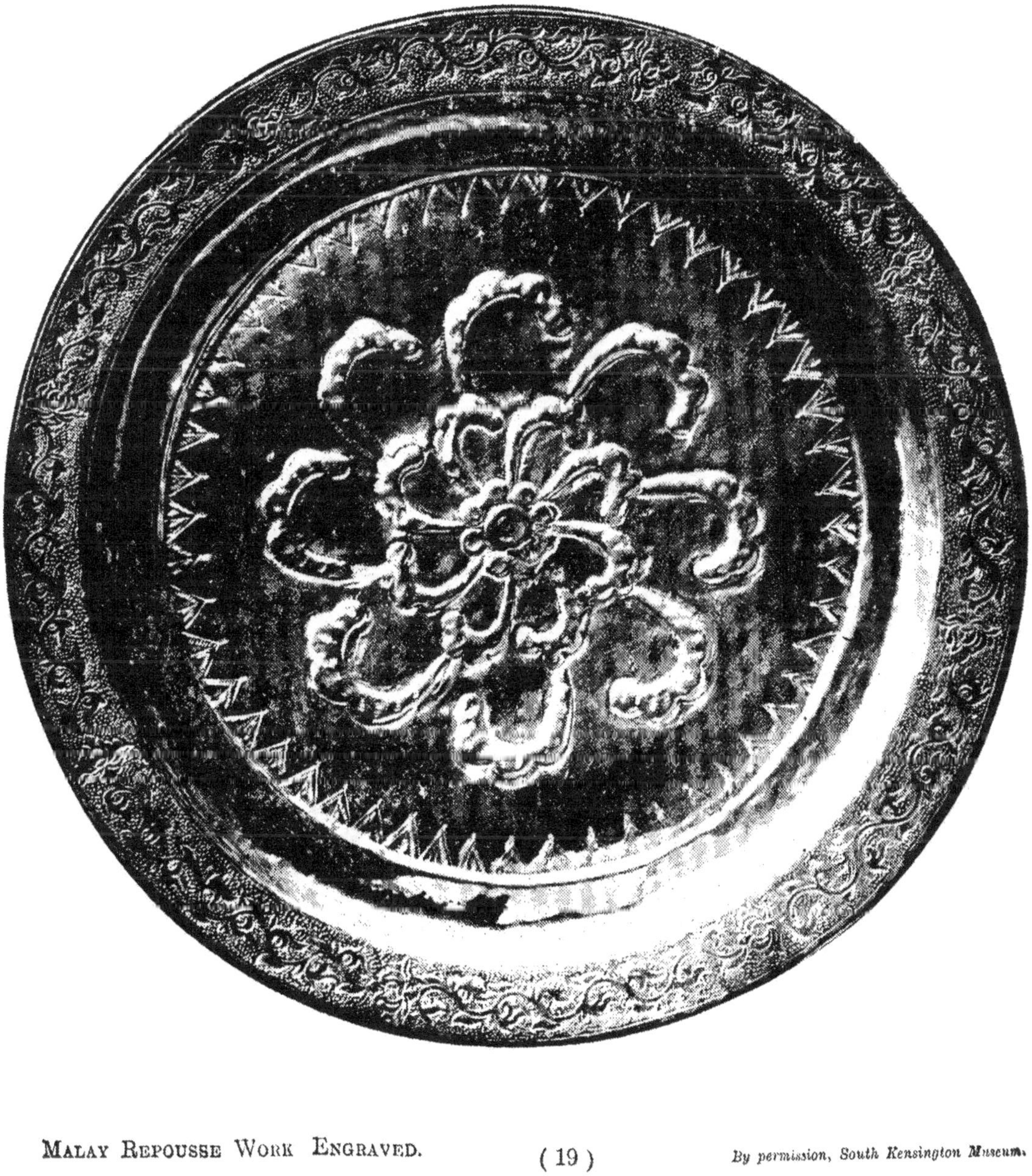

MALAY REPOUSSE WORK ENGRAVED. (19) By permission, South Kensington Museum.

PLATE III.

INDIAN LACE,

Square of White Lace, made at the Mission School, Tinnevelli.   Modern.

STAGE I.—Set out the square about 11 inches wide; draw diameter and diagonals. Set out the second square in due proportion to the large one to bear the centre of the wheels; next the octagon and then the star form in the middle. The size of all these divisions must be most accurately found; for instance, the tips of the star form are about half way between the centre and the edges of the square.

STAGE II.—The smaller divisions should be set out next.

STAGE III.—Fill in the detail, and give particularly care to Radiation in the wheels and the threads joining the wheels to the arcs. The leaf forms in the star must be made quite symmetrical; the thick portions are represented by double lines.

N.B.—This is a very clear case where no notice is to be taken of distortions owing to uneven stretching, or the irregularity of forms due to limitations of the materials. An intricate piece of work such as this should be left in outline, no attempt whatever being made to wash in a background.

PLATE III.

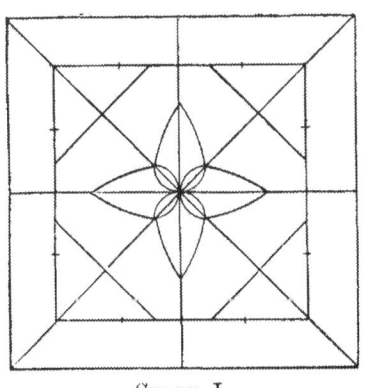

STAGE I.

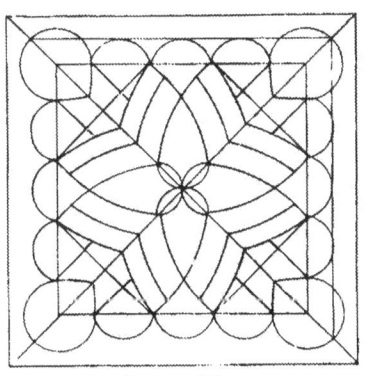

STAGE II.

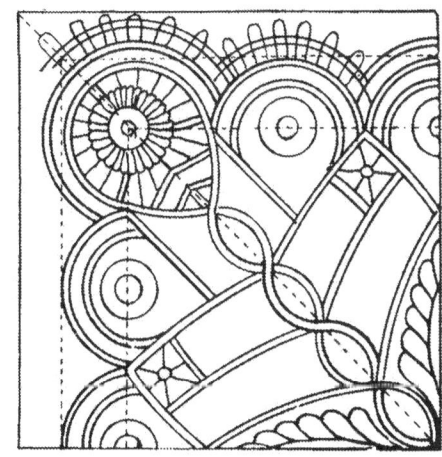

STAGE III.

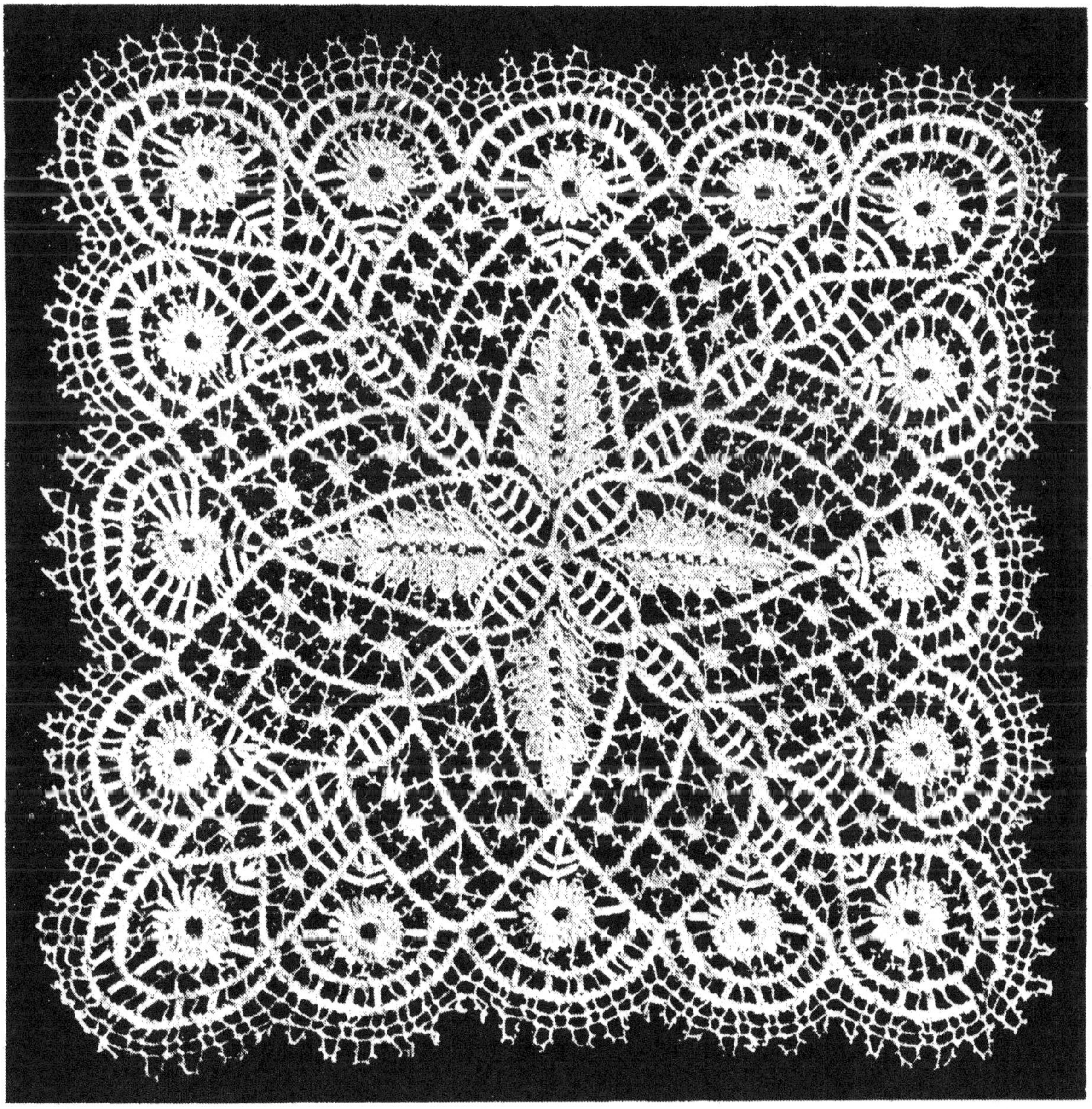

SQUARE OF INDIAN LACE. MODERN.

By permission, South Kensington Museum.

PLATE IV,

SYRIAN DISH

Painted China. Design a Dark Greenish Blue on a very Pale Ground of the same Colour. The Ornamental Scroll Work was evidently scratched with a Stylus while the Colour was wet. The Design in the Light Panels consists entirely of Brush Strokes.

STAGE I.—Carefully set out the circles in proper proportion to each other after drawing the eight diameters. Then draw the two squares as shown.

STAGE II.—Next draw the panels, whose sides you will observe do not quite fall upon the lines of the squares.

STAGE III.—It would be good practice to try to draw the ornamental forms in the panels, with the brush only. A few leading lines in pencil might be drawn first. Give particular care to radiation especially in the centre circular panel.

PLATE IV.

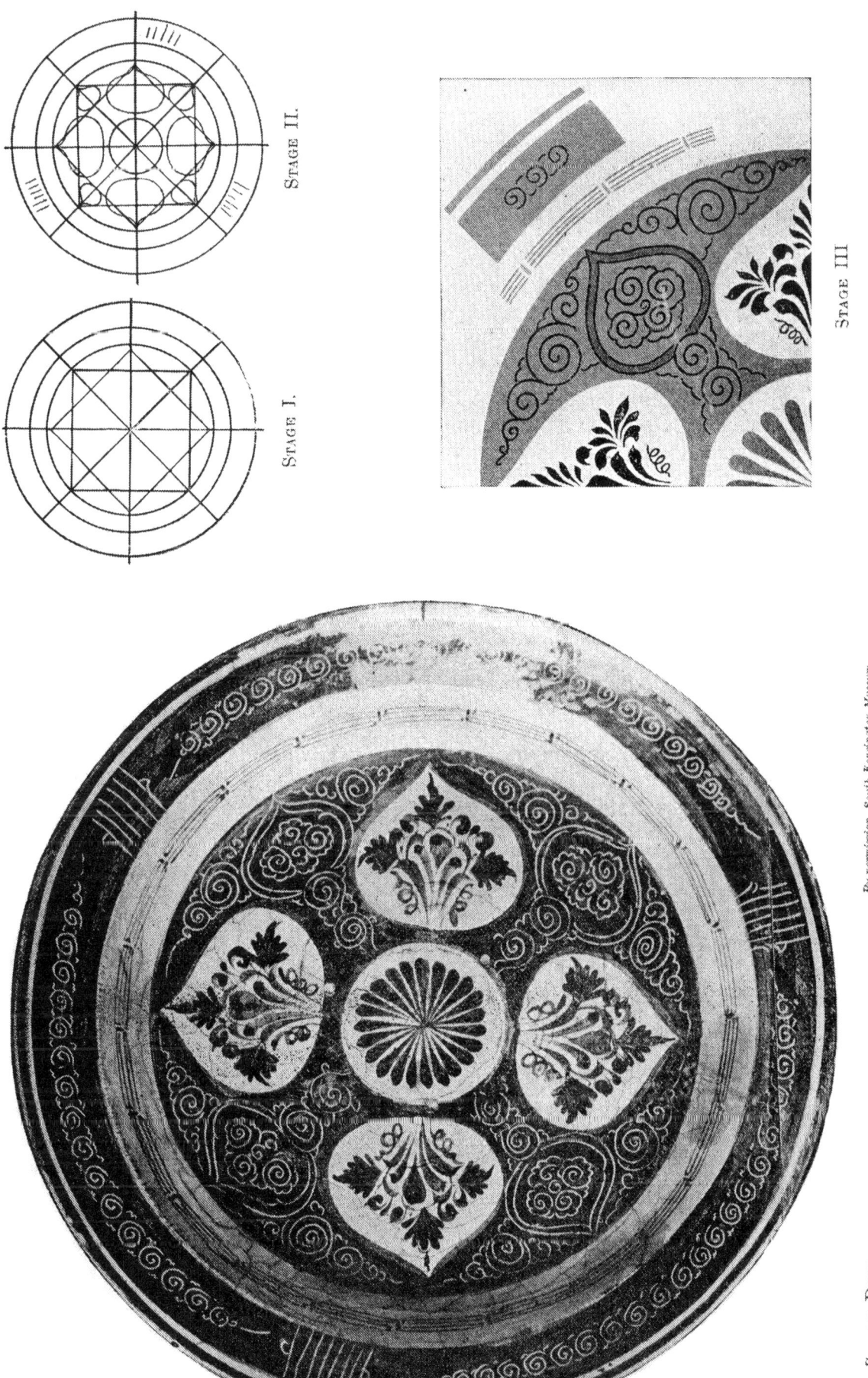

STAGE II.

STAGE I.

STAGE III

By permission. South Kensington Museum.

SYRIAN DISH.

PLATE V.

PORTION OF A CHIMNEY PIECE.

Inlay of Green White, and Red Marble. Milanese, about 1600.

STAGE I.—Set out the rectangle in proper proportion. Next draw the leading lines and carefully note the position of the binds.

STAGE II.—Draw the shape of the large masses.

STAGE III.—Fill in the details and line in with pen or brush. A wash of very dilute ink can be added as shown.

PLATE V.

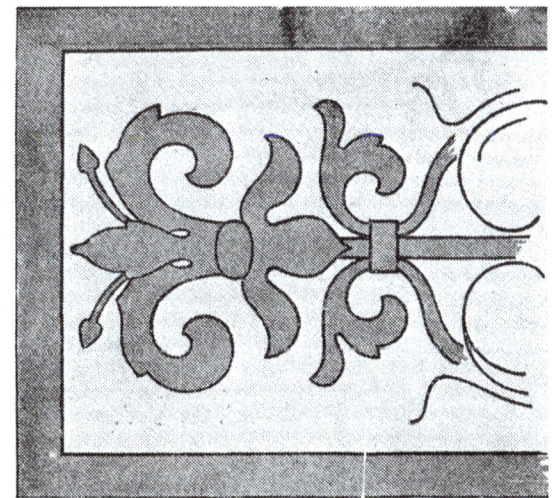

STAGE III.

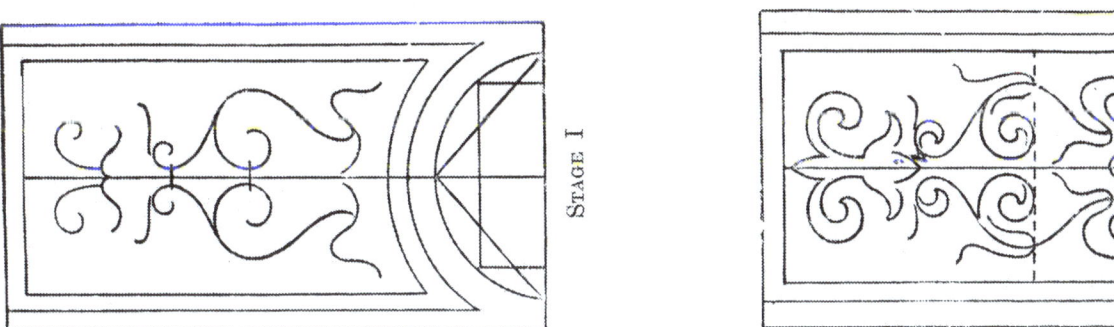

STAGE I

STAGE II.

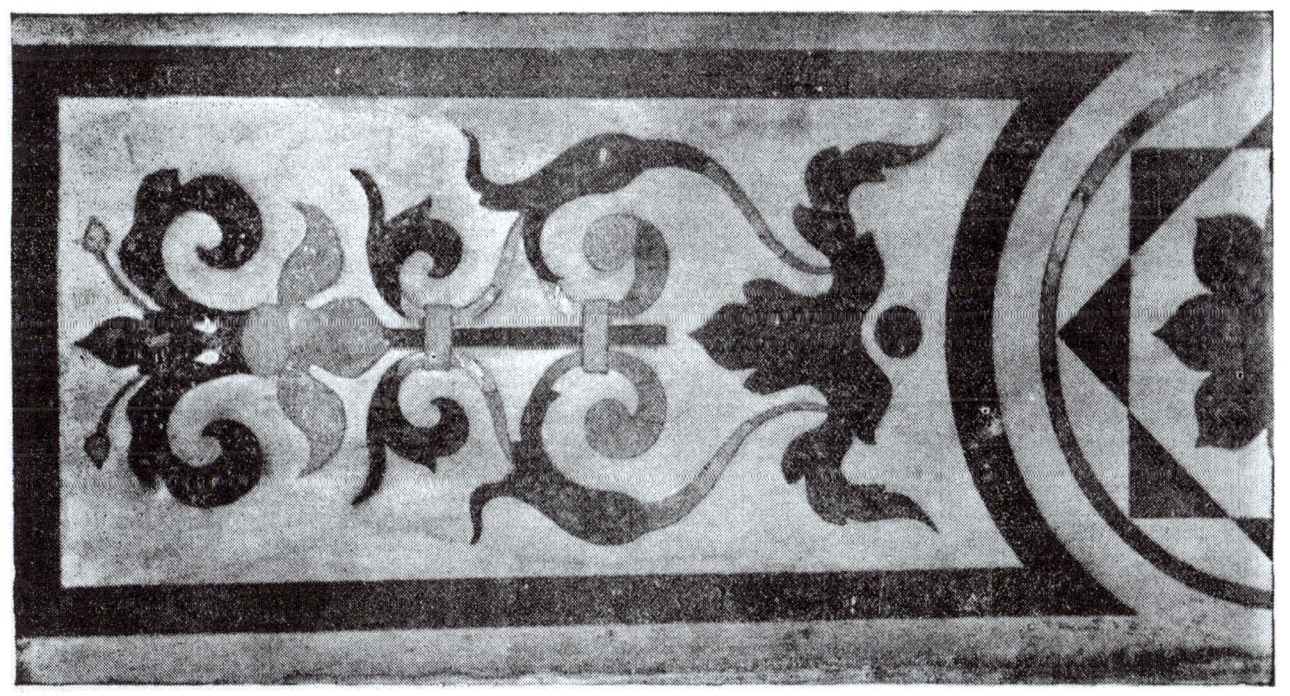

PORTION OF CHIMNEY PIECE. MILANESE.

By permission, South Kensington Museum.

PLATE VI.

APPAREL FOR SLEEVE OF A DALMATIC

Silk Velvet of Royal Blue Colour, Applique in Satin. French, 16th Century.

STAGE I.—Set out rectangle in due proportion and draw leading lines.

STAGE II.—Add "blocks" as shown. Read the chapter on Acanthus forms before filling the leaf forms into the blocks.

STAGE III.—Draw all the Acanthus forms completely. Line in with pen or brush. Double the outline as shown to represent the "cord" round the edges of the design. A wash of very dilute ink can be added.

PLATE VI.

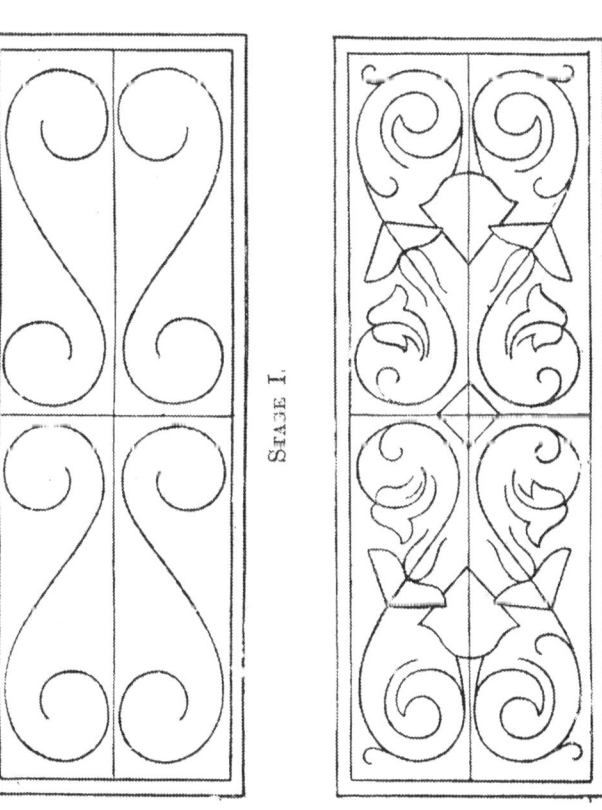

STAGE III.

STAGE I.

STAGE II.

By permission, South Kensington Museum.

APPAREL FOR A DALMATIC. APPLIQUÉ. FRENCH, 16TH CENTURY.

PLATE VII.

EMBROIDERED BORDER.

Border of a Canopy, Delhi. Ground of Peacock Blue, embroidered with Gold Thread.

STAGE I.—Set out the rectangle in proper proportions; next space out the bands at the top and bottom; and fill in the leading lines which are based upon a wave *motive*.

STAGE II.—Fill in the "blocks" to contain the rosettes, and also add the secondary leading lines. Divide up the circle for the petals of the rosettes.

STAGE III.—Draw the forms carefully as shown and add a wash of very dilute ink if required. The portion completed is sufficient for Examination purposes.

N.B.—No notice must be taken of the uneven stretching of the material as seen in the bottom band, where the forms are somewhat distorted.

PLATE VII.

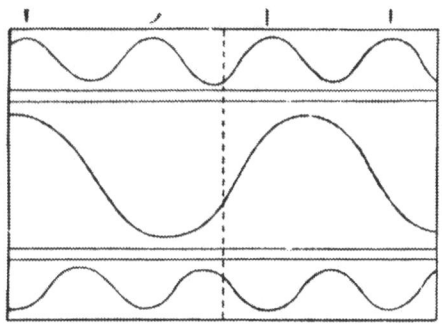

STAGE I.

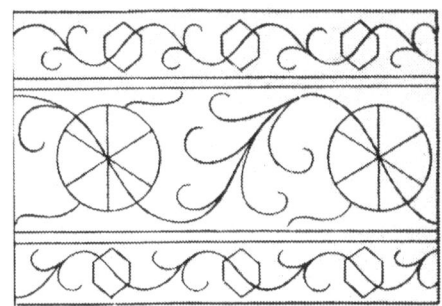

STAGE II.

STAGE III

EMBROIDERED BORDER OF A CANOPY, DELHI.

By permission, South Kensington Museum.

(29)

PLATE VIII.

SILK BROCADE.

Silk Brocade. Red, Pink, and White Flowers on a White Damask Ground. French, Lyons, 1750.

STAGE I.—Set out the rectangle in proper proportion, and draw the leading lines.

STAGE II.—Notice particularly which part of the copy falls on a line half way down the photograph. When filling in the "blocks" great care must be given to see that they are in the right position and of the right size.

STAGE III.—Examples of how to render the blossoms, buds and leaves are given. The *character* of the petals must be preserved by keeping their shape thus ⋂ not ⋂ . The stems are to be drawn quite smoothly no notice being taken of their saw-like character which is owing to the woven nature of the material.

PLATE VIII.

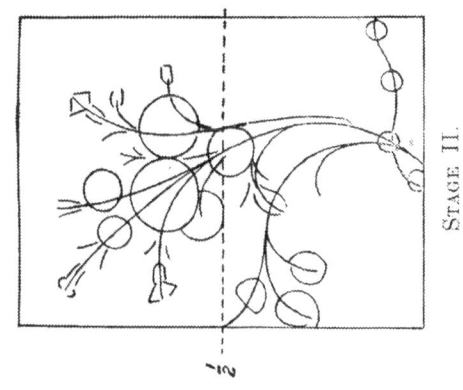

STAGE II.

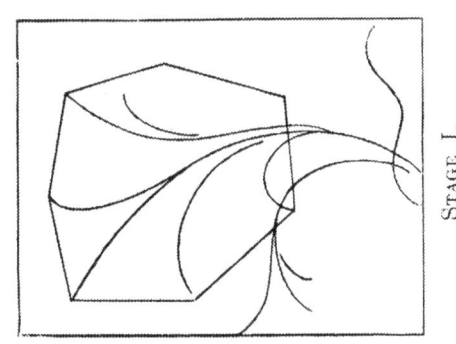

STAGE I.

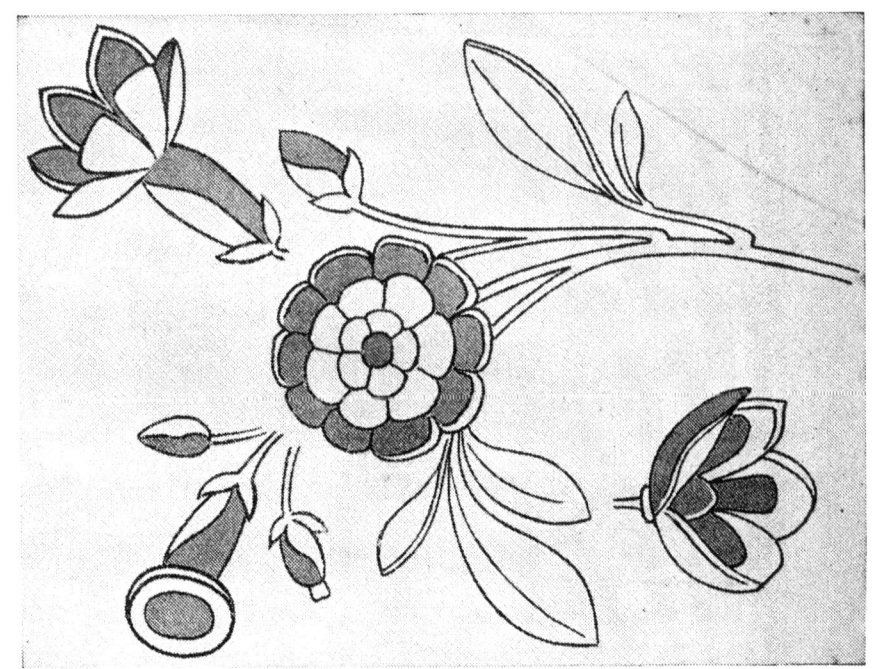

STAGE III

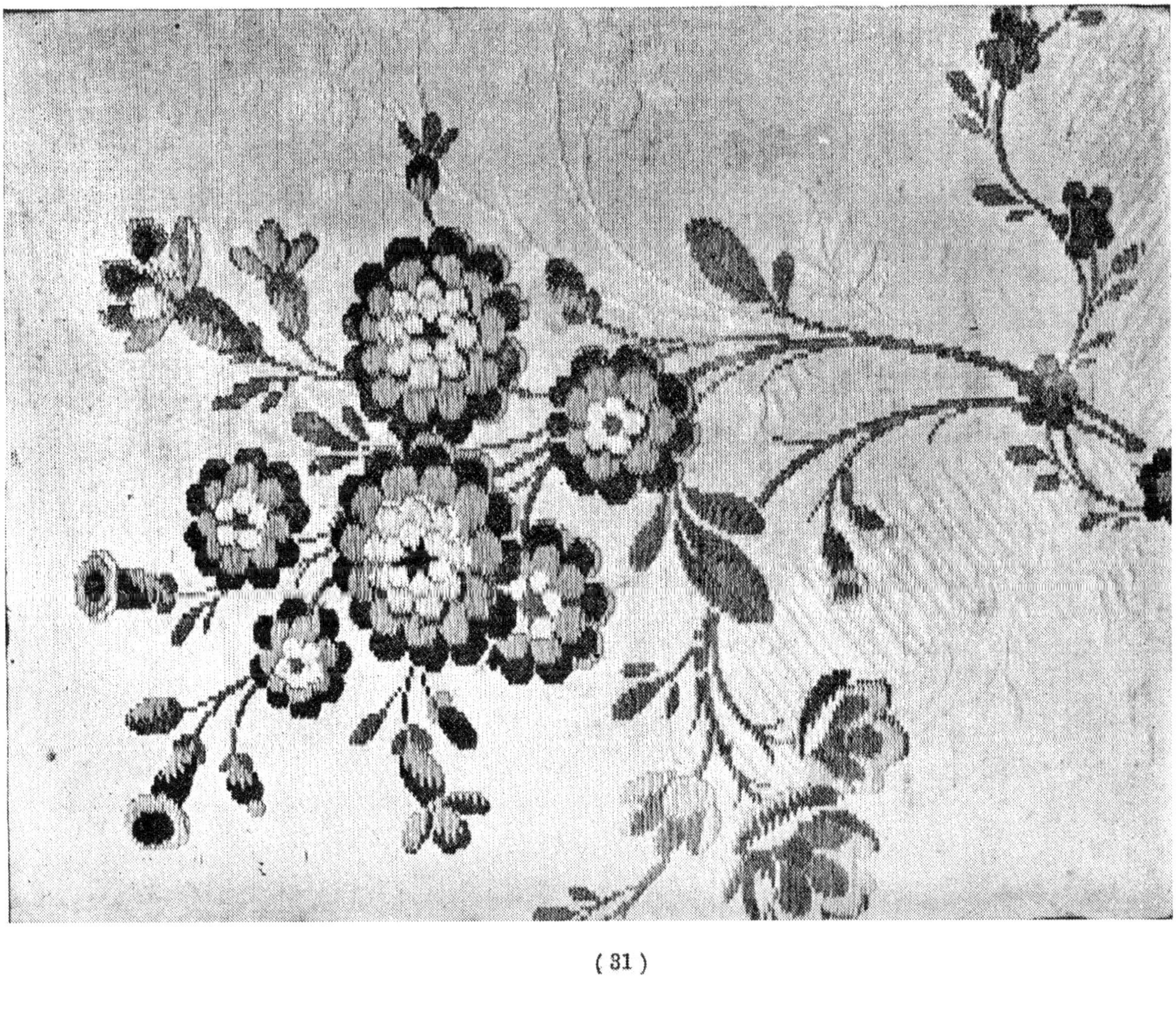

By permission, South Kensington Museum.

SILK BROCADE. FRENCH, LYONS 1750.

PLATE IX.

PORTION OF AN ORPHREY

Ground Green Velvet, Applique of Yellow Silk and Gold Thread.   French or Spanish,

---

STAGE I.—After setting out the rectangle, space out the borders at each side. Notice that their width is greater than appears at first sight. They are about one-fifth the total width. Note also which form falls on the half way line.

STAGE II.—Draw the "blocks" as shown taking care to fill up the spaces well. Notice the *nearness* of one form to another.

STAGE III.—Be very careful when drawing the Acanthus forms in the leaves. Practise drawing "lines of beauty" at every opportunity. The *cord* round the edges is represented by doubling the outline as shown. A wash can be added at option.

N.B.—The mid-rib omitted on the Acanthus leaf in Diagram III. must be shown as a double line in the finished drawing.

PLATE IX.

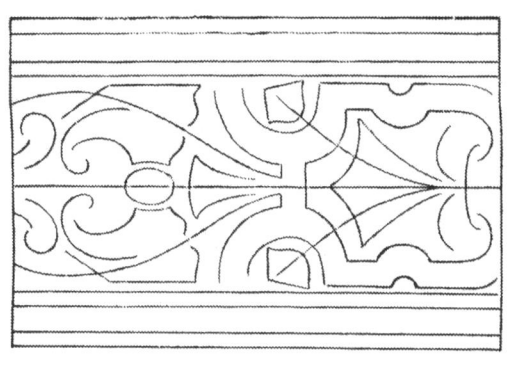

STAGE II.

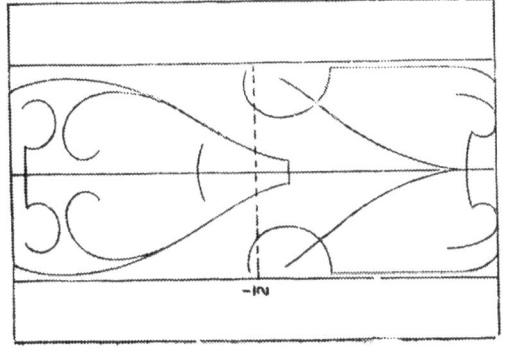

STAGE I.

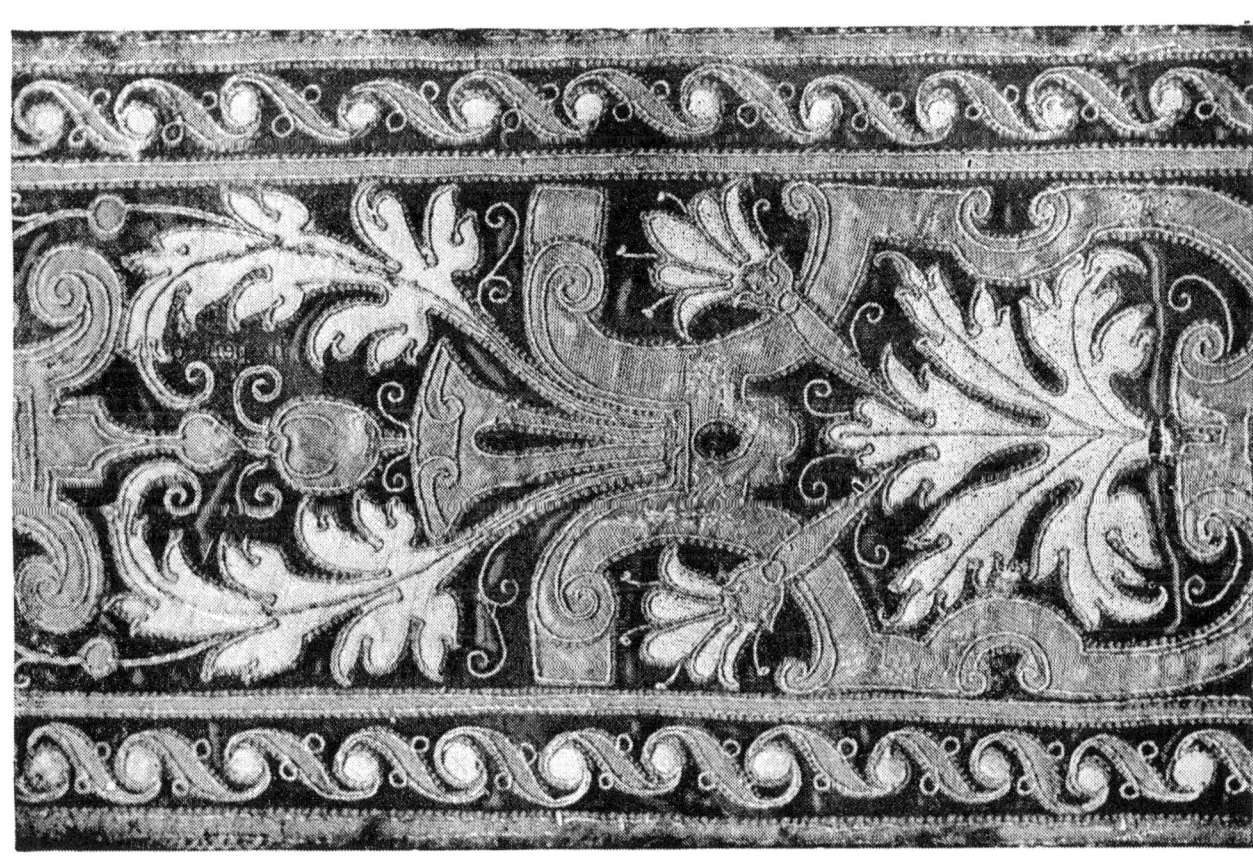

STAGE III.

PORTION OF AN ORPHREY.   FRENCH OR SPANISH.   *By permission, South Kensington Museum.*

PLATE X.

CHAIR BACK.

Embroidered Crimson Velvet, Applique in Corded Silk, edged with Gold Cord.

STAGE I.—After setting out the rectangle give special care to the correct spacing of the bands, top and bottom; then draw the leading lines.

STAGE II.—Add the wave motive in the bands, and the "blocks" to the design. Note carefully the nearness of one form to another.

STAGE III.—Add the details giving great care to the Acanthus forms. The cord is represented by doubling the outline. Line in with pen or brush and add a wash if so desired.

N.B.—No accidents are to be drawn. Make both ends alike. Do no finishing work to the border until the whole design is done in the panel.

PLATE X.

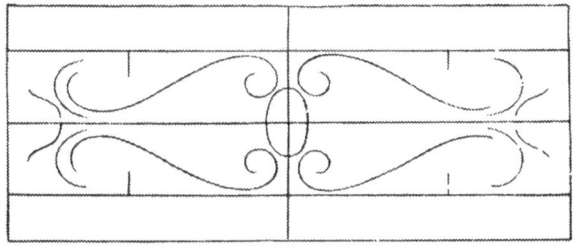

STAGE I.

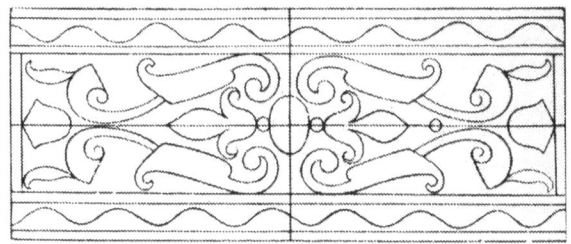

STAGE II

STAGE III.

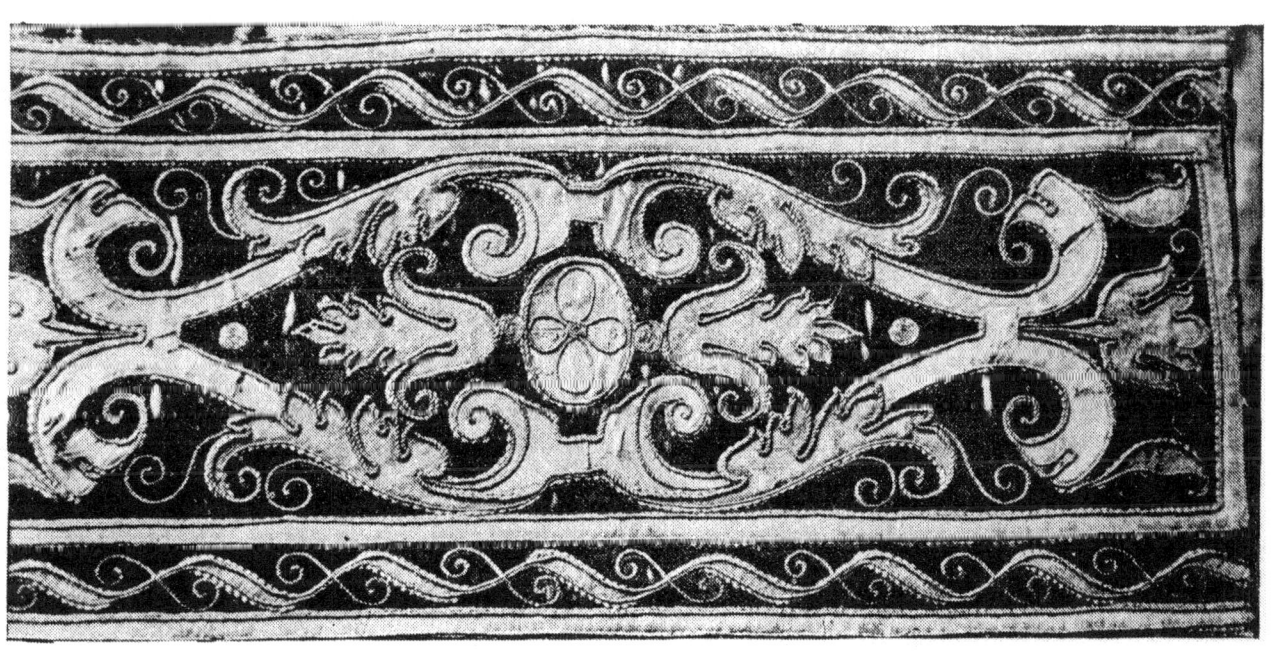

CHAIR BACK. APPLIQUE. PROBABLY FRENCH.

By permission, South Kensington Museum.

(35)

PLATE XI.

EMBROIDERED VELVET

Piece of Crimson Velvet embroidered in Coloured Silks.

STAGE I.—Great care must be given to the proportions of the rectangle. Notice how many times the height measures along the length. Find the relative position of point A most carefully. Draw the leading lines.

STAGE II.—The blocks are small and many. See that each one occupies the right amount of space and notice the *nearness* of one form to another.

STAGE III.—Acanthus forms abound in this. The markings on the Dolphins as well as the serrations in the leaves are composed of *lines of beauty*. Read up the chapter on Acanthus forms before finishing this with the brush. No background has been washed in so that an example may be shown of outline only.

PLATE XI.

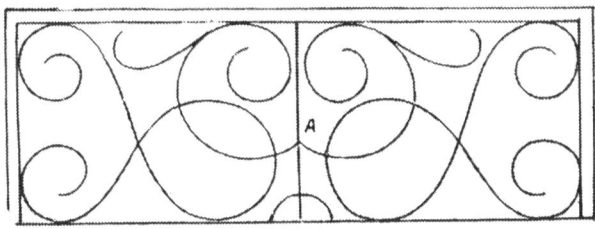

STAGE I.

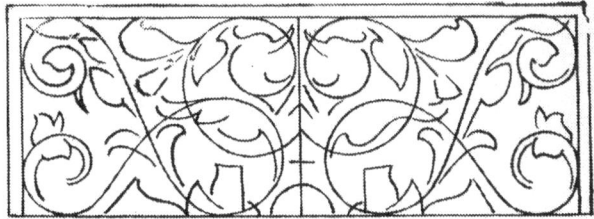

STAGE II.

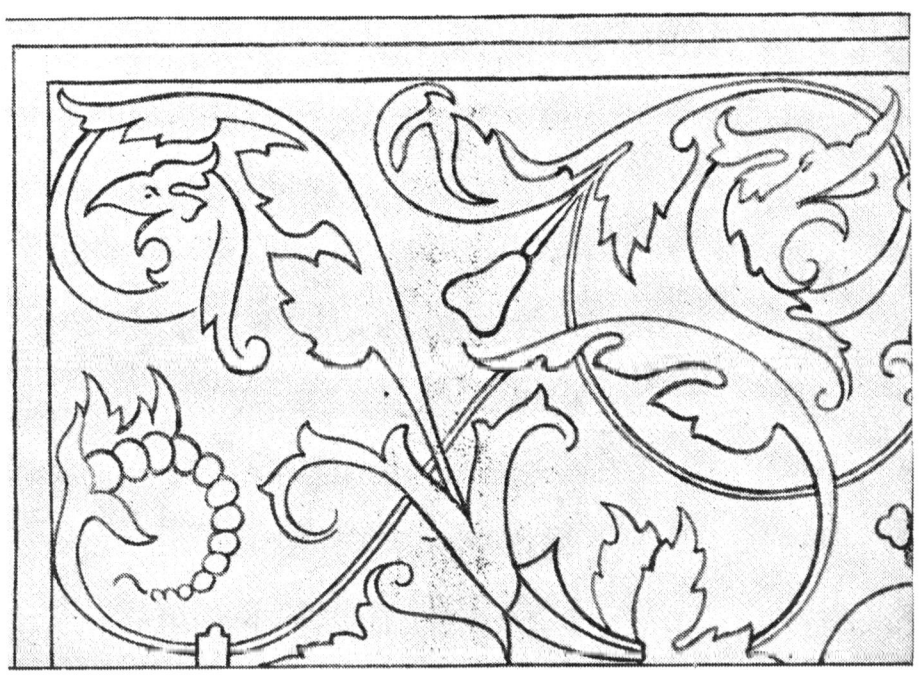

STAGE III

PIECE OF EMBROIDERED VELVET.

Part of Copy set at South Kensington Exam., June, 1904.

(37)

PLATE XII.

PANEL OF A BOX

Marquetry of Ivory and Tortoise-shell.   Italian 17th Century.

STAGE I.—Set out the proportions of the panel very carefully. Then draw the leading lines as shown.

STAGE II.—Fill in the blocks as shown, keeping them full large. The tendency in this copy is to make the blocks small.

STAGE III.—Fill in all the smaller forms giving great attention to *tangential junction.* Read the chapter on Radiation and Tangential Junction. A wash has been added here up to the pencil lines, and then cleaned up, leaving simply the white forms without outline. This is known as "silhouette" troatmont.

PLATE XII

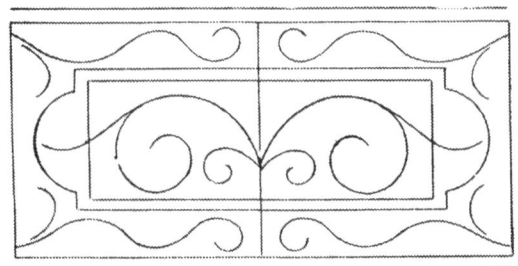

STAGE I.

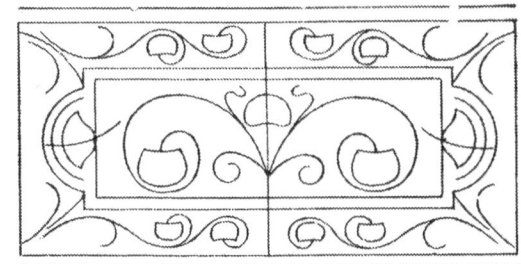

STAGE II.

STAGE III.

IVORY INLAY. ITALIAN.   (39)   *By permission, South Kensington Museum.*

PLATE XIII.

CARVED PANEL.

Part of a Panel of Red Sandstone with Arabesques and Foliated Carved Ornament, from the Birbal's Palace at Fathpur Sikri. Mogul 16th Century.

STAGE I.—Set out the rectangle with its border and add the geometry construction (Motive of squares set diamond-wise).

STAGE II.—Add the *leading lines*, working upon the motive as shown.

STAGE III.—Draw all the forms all over the copy before finishing a part as shown. This is an example of *Relief*. Read the section of the Introduction dealing with that subject. Note that the upper edges are dark and strong and the lower edges a little lighter. In relief work no background is required. Outline is quite sufficient.

PLATE XIII.

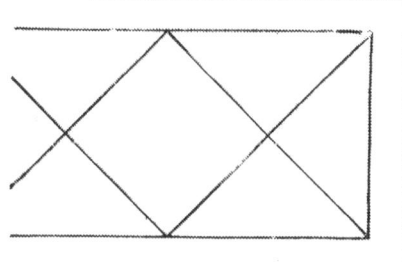

STAGE I.

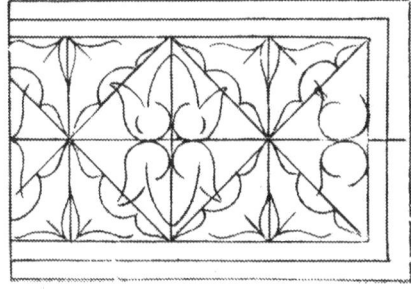

STAGE II.

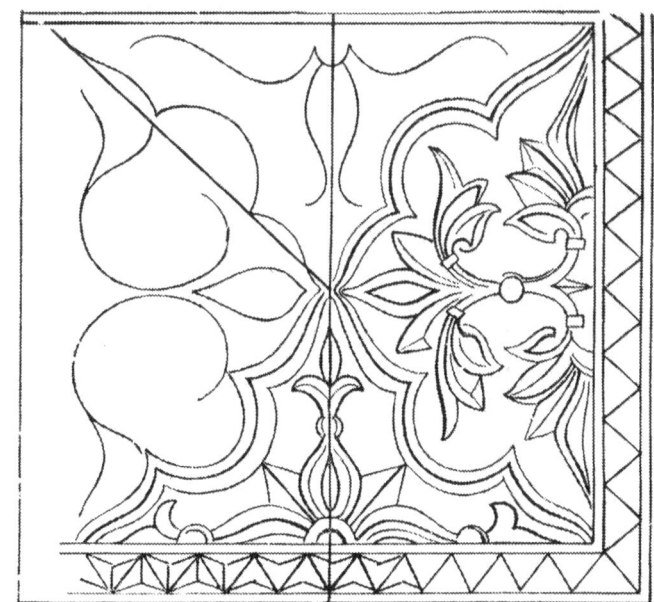

STAGE III.

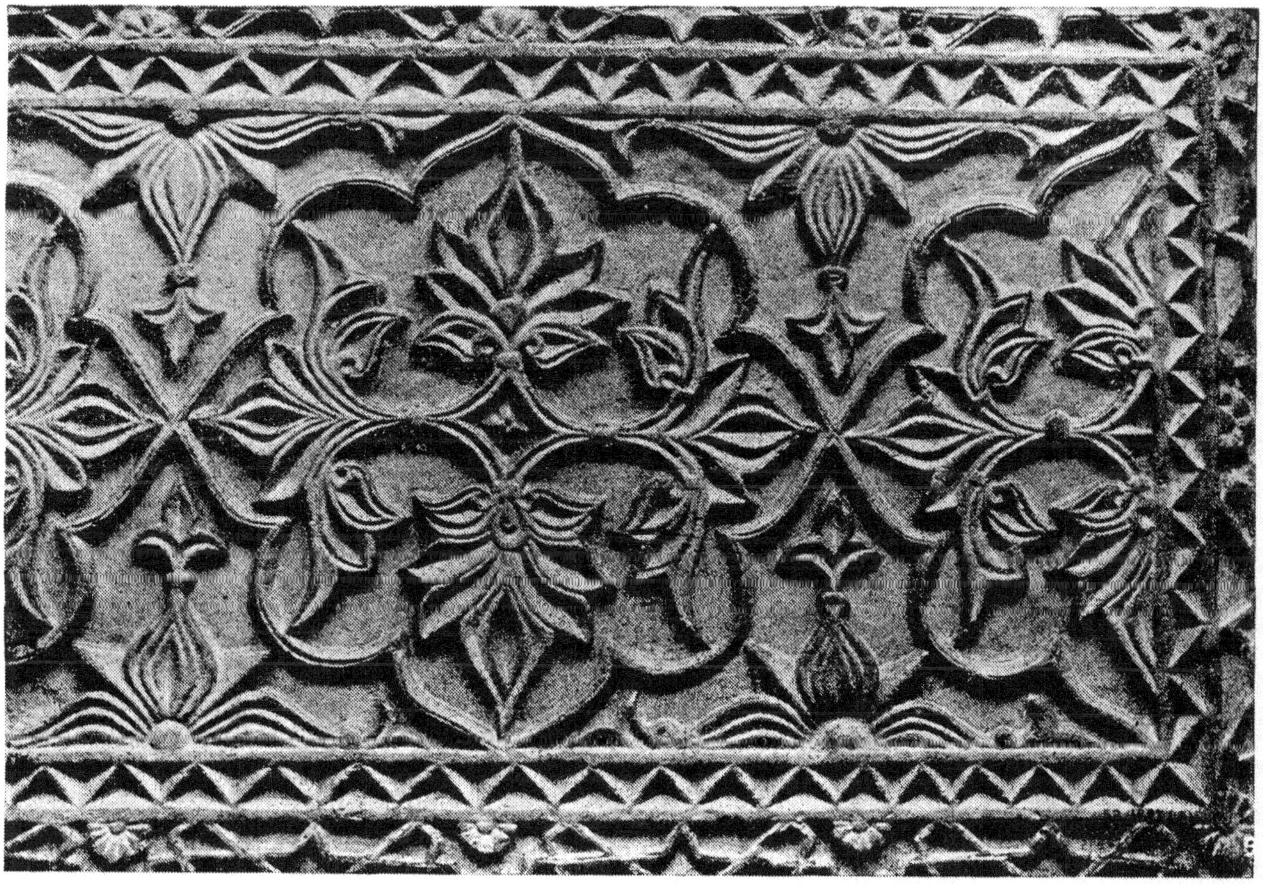

PANEL, BIRBAL'S PALACE. MOGUL WORK, 16TH CENTURY.

y permission, South Kensington Museum.

PLATE XIV

LINTEL OF A MANTELPIECE

Carved Stone.   Design based upon the VINE.   From the Old Palace, Bromley-by-Bow.

STAGE I.—Draw the rectangle, and carefully space out the borders top and bottom in proper proportion. Draw the leading lines as shown.

STAGE II.—Add the blocks for the leaves, bunches of grapes, and the spirals of tendrils.

STAGE III—This is another example of Relief. Notice that the grapes are not *round*, but partake somewhat of the hexagonal form. This gives the character of their being pressed one against another.

PLATE XIV.

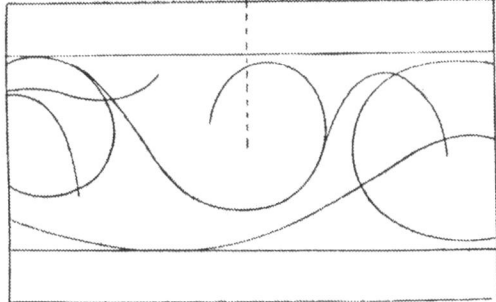

STAGE I.

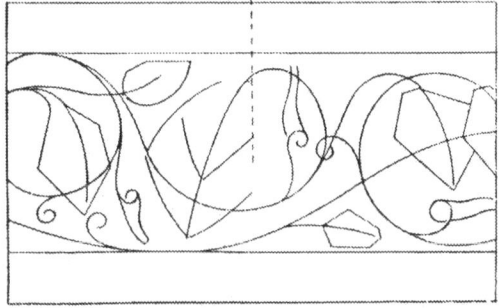

STAGE II.

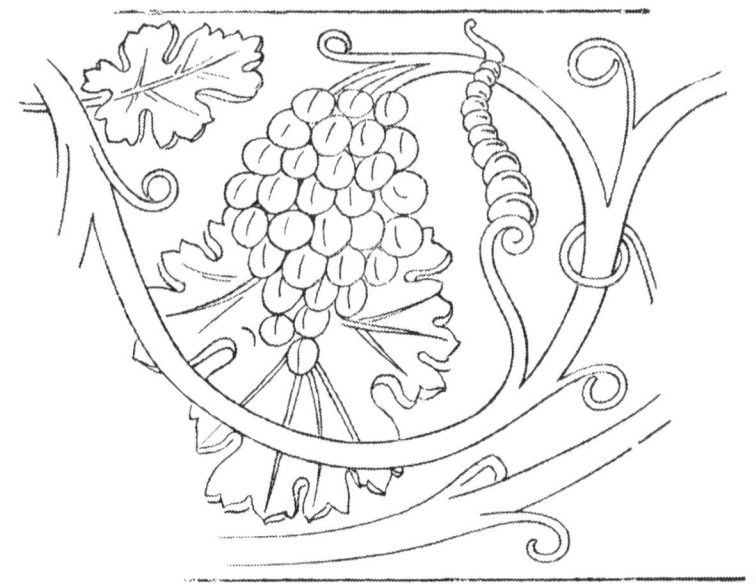

STAGE III.

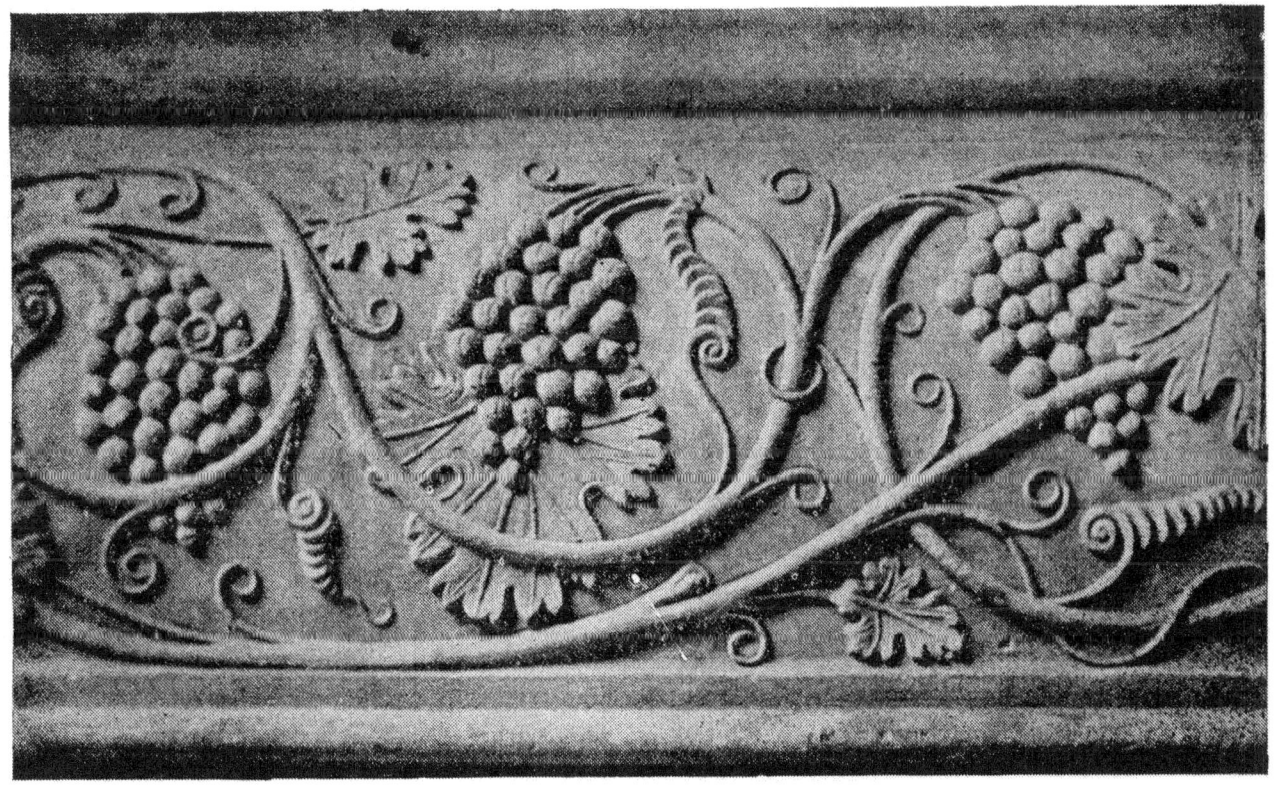

PORTION OF A LINTEL OVER A FIRE PLACE.   OLD PALACE, BROMLEY-BY-BOW.   *By permission, South Kensington Museum.*

PLATE XV.

WROUGHT IRON BRACKET

Wrought Iron.   Modern.

STAGE I.—Set the bracket out at right angles noting the proportion of B C to B D.   Then carefully find point A about half way down the bracket, and draw the leading lines.

STAGE II.—Add the smaller curves and the two blocks to contain the foliage.

STAGE III.—Treat this similarly to the relief ornament.   In showing the thickness of the scrolls and the foliage, make the upper edges strong and dark and the lower ones a little lighter.

N.B.—Owing to the foreshortening of the bracket in the photograph the top left hand corner has come out an obtuse angle, instead of a right angle as it should be.

PLATE XV.

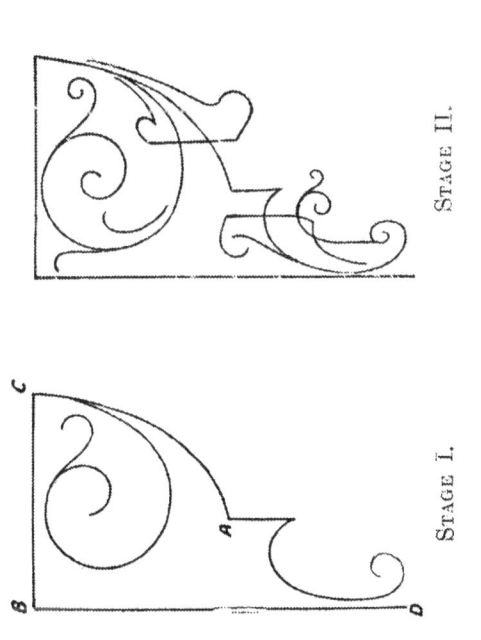

STAGE II.

STAGE I.

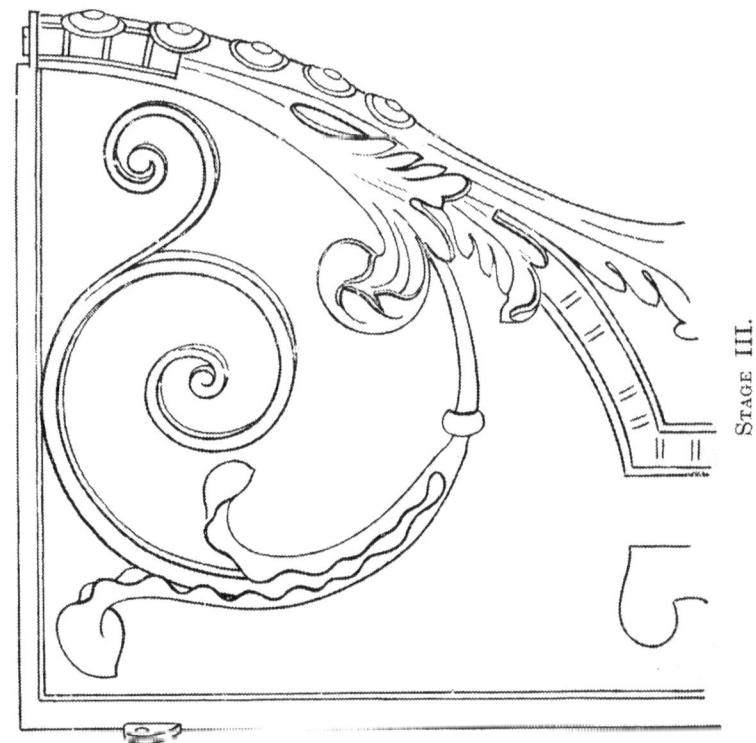

STAGE III.

WROUGHT IRON BRACKET. MODERN. *By permission, South Kensington Museum*

PLATE XVI.

A PIECE OF CARVING.

Set at the King's Scholarship Examination, December, 1904.

STAGE I.—Set out the relative height and width of the copy. The width will be found to be 1½ times the height. Next find position of important points such as A, and B B, C and D. Point A is found to be a little more than half way up. B and B are practically on a level with A. Next it will be noticed that C and D are each about one-third along width. Draw the leading lines as shown.

STAGE II.—Block out the general shape of the *masses* using as many straight lines as possible. Observe the photo carefully for these straight-lined forms.

STAGE III.—Before setting out the *lobes* of each leaf as shown, read up the hints on "Acanthus Forms." The position of the *eyes* must be carefully noted and then the enclosing lobes drawn, after which they are again broken up by drawing the serrations (Stage 4.)

STAGE IV.—First read up Hints on "*Relief*," then put in the serrations and lastly the relief as shown. Note carefully the *radiation* of all the *veins* and *pipes* from the mid-rib. The beads composing the mid-rib need not all be drawn but only indicated. Particularly note that they are not round, but irregular in form (really small octagons) due to pressure.

In principles of ornament, this copy is a good example of *Balance, i.e.,* the two halves correspond in *weight* and *mass* but are not both exactly alike; the copy is not symmetrical.

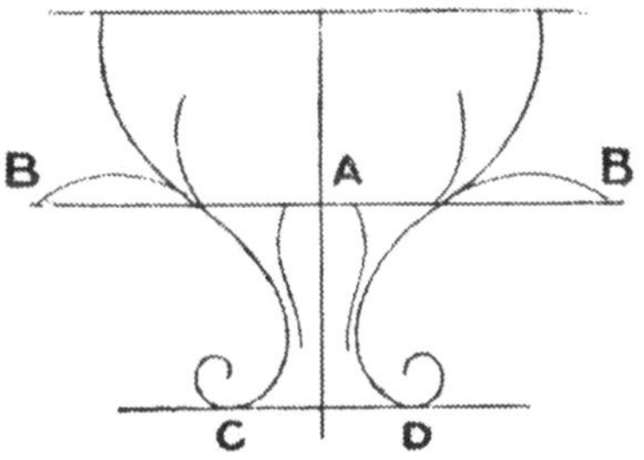

PLATE XVI.

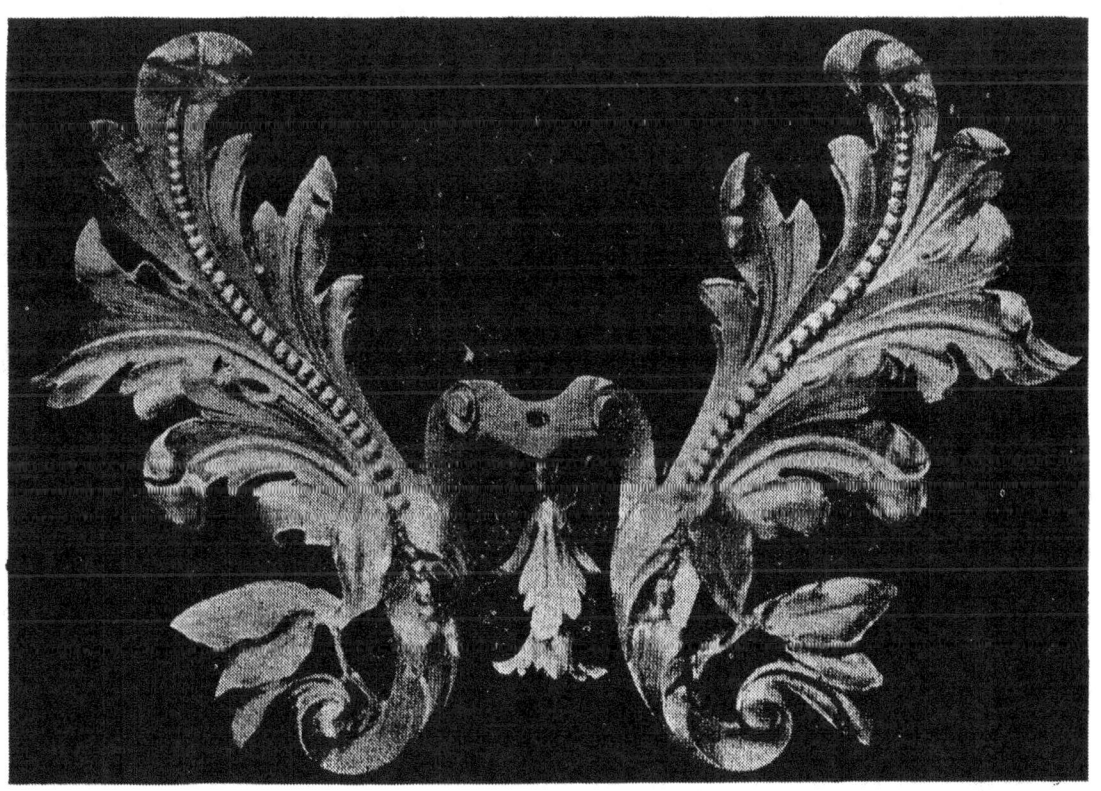

STAGE I.

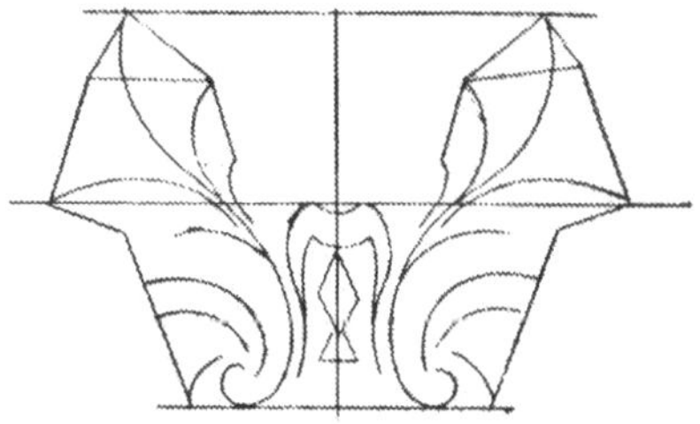

STAGE II.

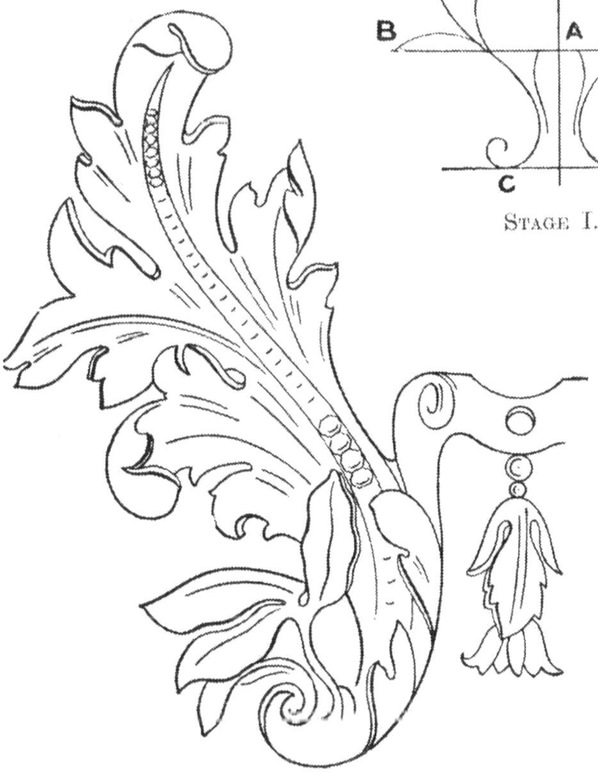

STAGE IV.

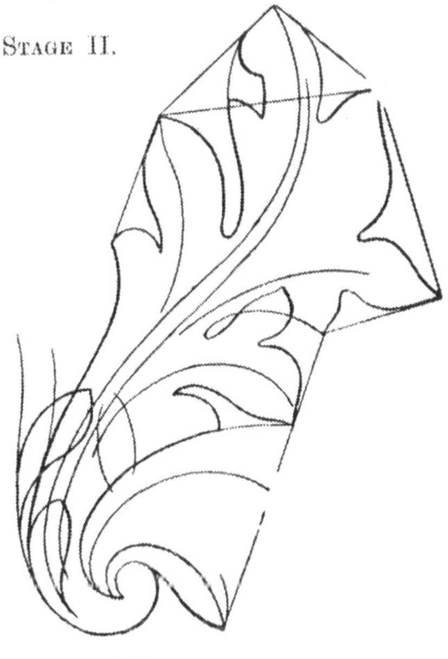

STAGE III.

A PIECE OF CARVING.

From Ralph's "Reprint of Scholarship Questions."

PLATE XVII.

CARVED FRAME.

Top of a Carved Frame of Stained Wood.   Italian 17th Century.

STAGE I.—Compare height with the length and set out the arc as shown. Divide each half into (say) three equal parts. This gives the positions of the important features. Draw the leading lines.

STAGE II.—Fill in the "blocks" as shown. The bird forms are indicated in each case by two main flowing curves; and the human head by a form composed of as many straight lines as possible.

STAGE III.—Before proceeding to the Relief, sketch in all the shapes of the leaves, wings, fruit, etc., and then finish off in the manner shown, giving great care to rendering the relief properly. Treat the birds in a very stiff and conventional manner, and do not attempt in the least to make them look like real birds. The features of the human face need only be indicated as shown in diagram 3.

PLATE XVII.

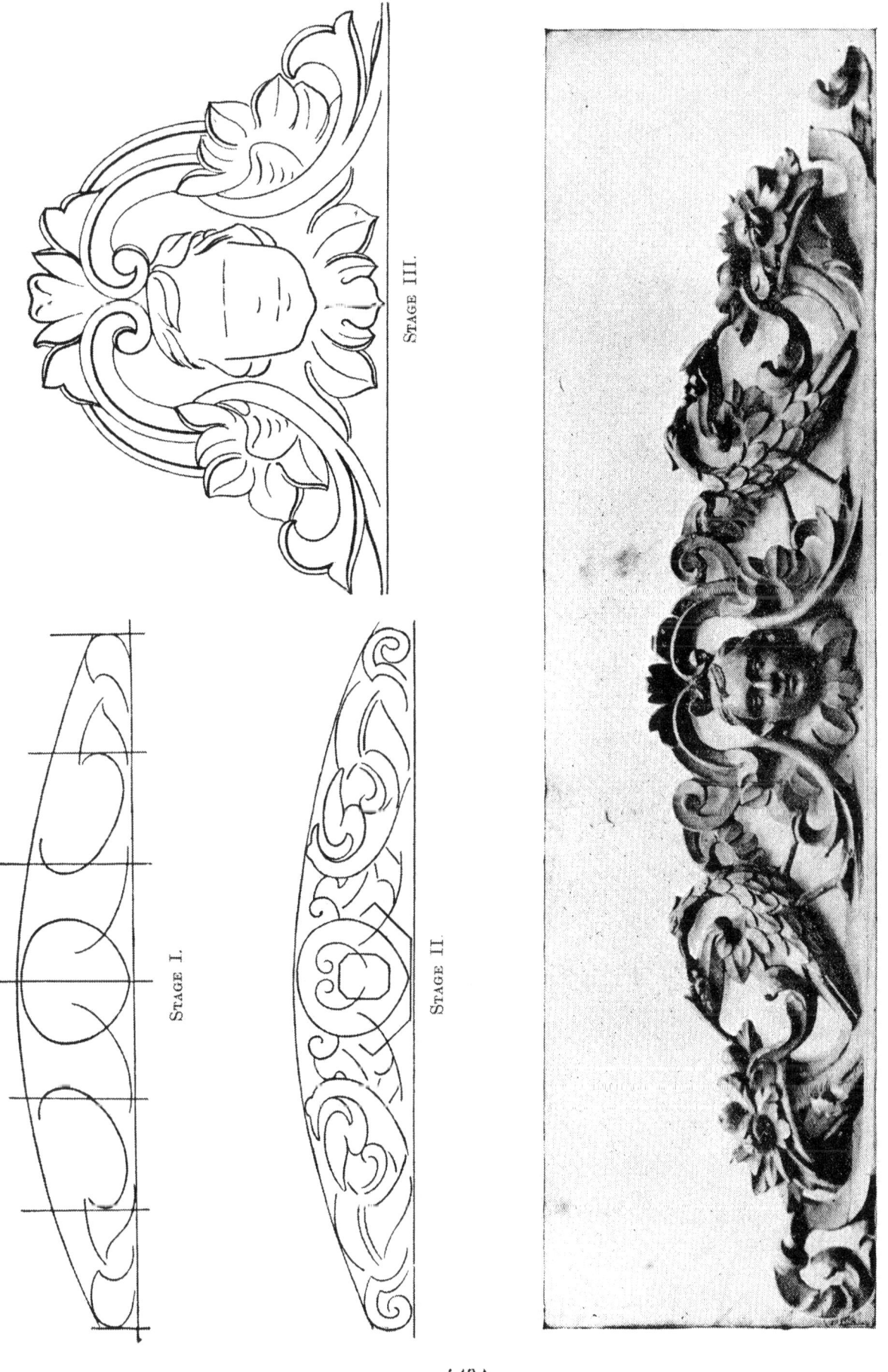

STAGE III.

STAGE I.

STAGE II.

By permission, South Kensington Museum.

MIRROR FRAME. ITALIAN 17TH CENTURY.

PLATE XVIII.

LINEN BORDER.

Linen worked in Red Silk, an S shaped pattern reversed alternately, enclosing Flowers and Leaves conventionally treated. South Italian 17th Century.

Stage I.—After setting out the bands top and bottom, draw the zig-zag motive shown enclosing the circles.

Stage II.—Fill in the blocks and notice their *nearness* one to another.

Stage III.—It is only necessary to complete *one repeat* as shown. The saw-like edges (owing to the nature of the work and material) are to be rendered as smooth continuous curves similar to Plate VIII. A careful study of this rendering will well repay the student.

PLATE XVIII.

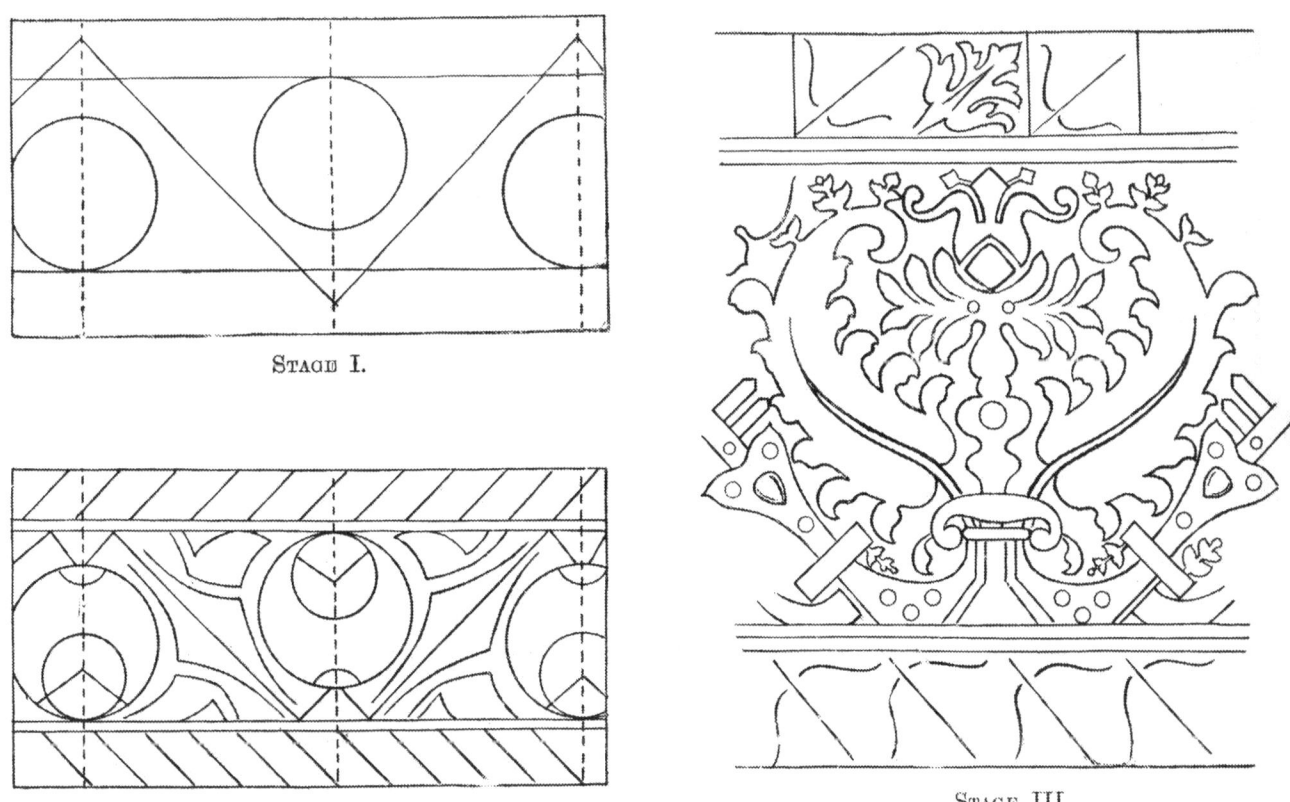

STAGE I.

STAGE II.

STAGE III.

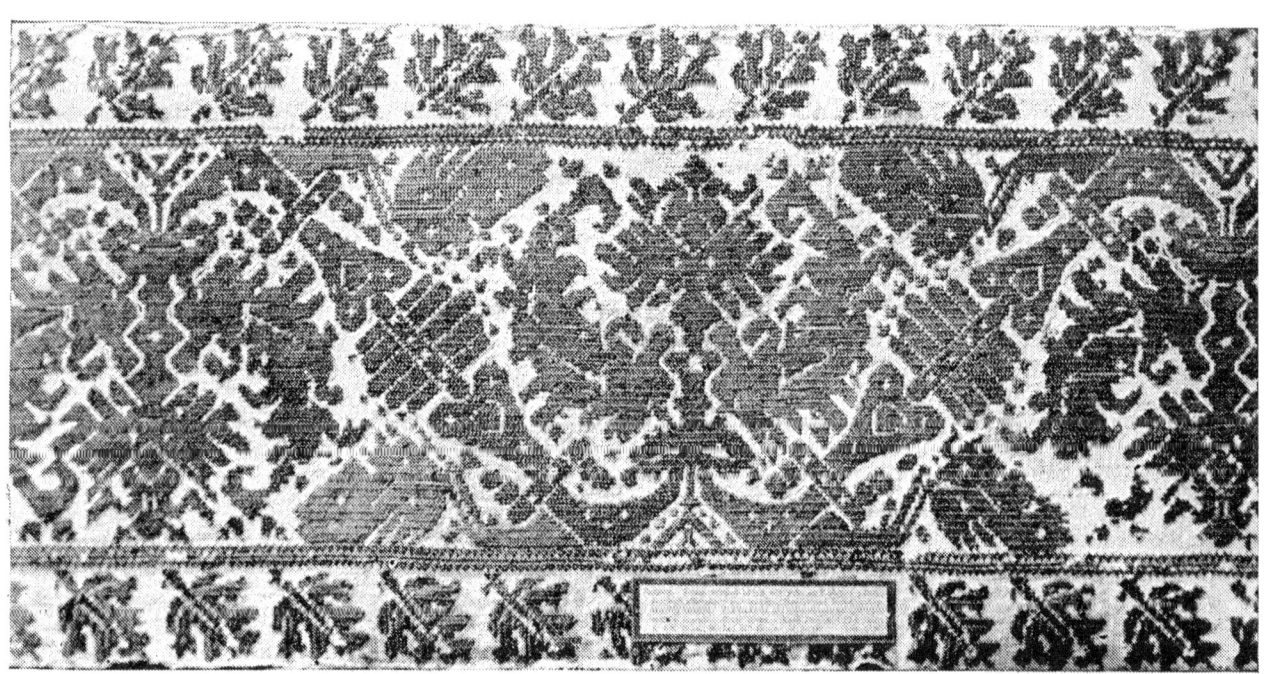

LINEN BORDER WORKED IN RED SILK. ITALIAN 17TH CENTURY.

By permission, South Kensington Museum.

(51)

PLATE XIX.

MARBLE INLAY.

Portion of Chimney Piece of Green, White and Red Marbles.   Milanese, 1600.

STAGE I.—Set out the rectangle as shown making both ends equal in width. (The inequality in the photograph is owing to foreshortening). Draw the leading lines, first marking the position of point A.

STAGE II.—Fill in all the blocks and notice the *nearness* of one form to another.

STAGE III.—Draw all the forms in pencil.   Read up the chapters on Acanthus Forms and Rectangularity before drawing the serrations in the leaves.   Then finish with pen or brush in a bold outline.   A wash may be added as shown.

PLATE XIX.

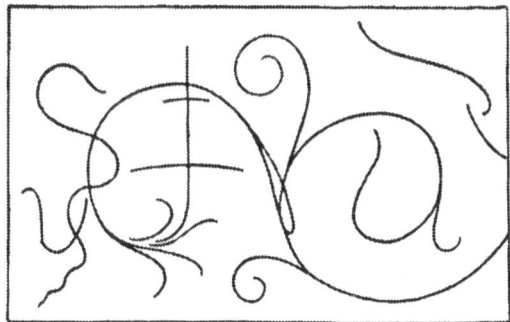

STAGE I.

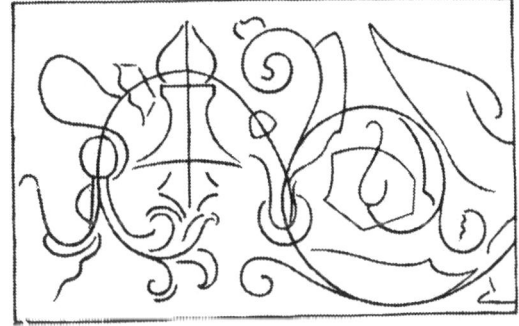

STAGE II.

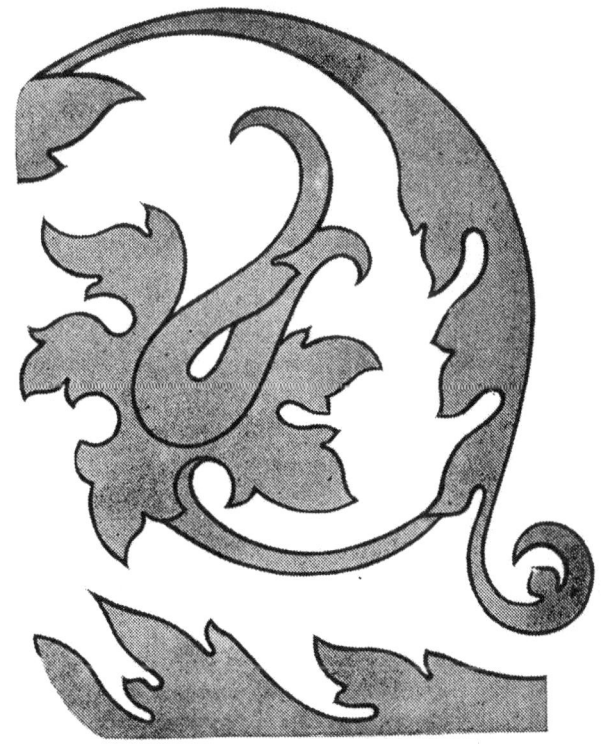

STAGE III.

MARBLE INLAY. MILANESE. 1600.

By permission, South Kensington Museum.

PLATE XX

WROUGHT IRON DESIGN.

Part of a Wrought Iron Gate.   Scroll and Strapwork.   German, about 1700.

STAGE I.—Compare full height with full width. Find positions of points A and B up the centre line. Draw the irregular figure C A D B. Next add the leading lines.

STAGE II.—Add the secondary curves and the few blocks.

STAGE III —Sketch all the strapwork and foliage, and restore where any is missing. Complete a small portion as shown similar in treatment to Plate XV.

N.B.—The whole design must be set at right angles, no notice being taken of the slight foreshortening.

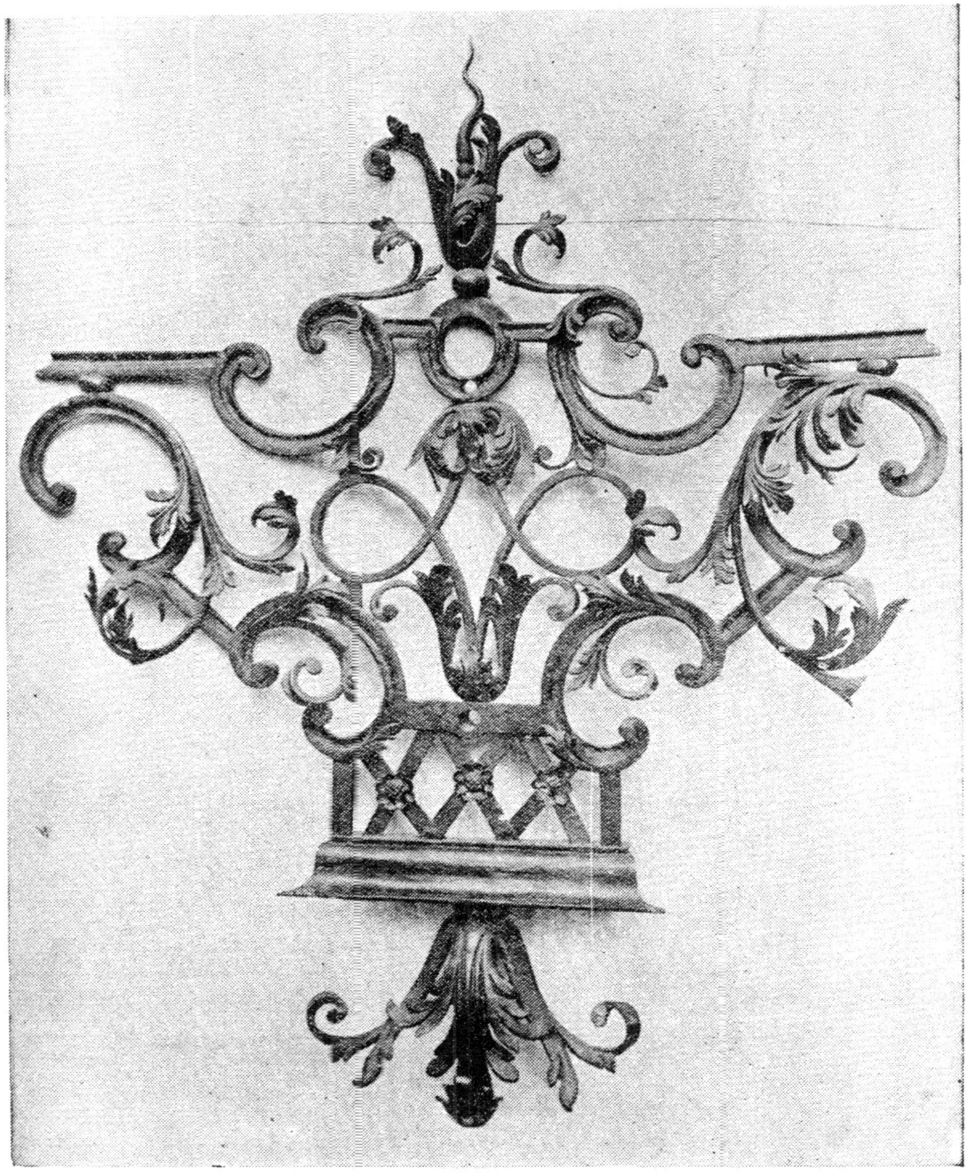

PLATE XX.

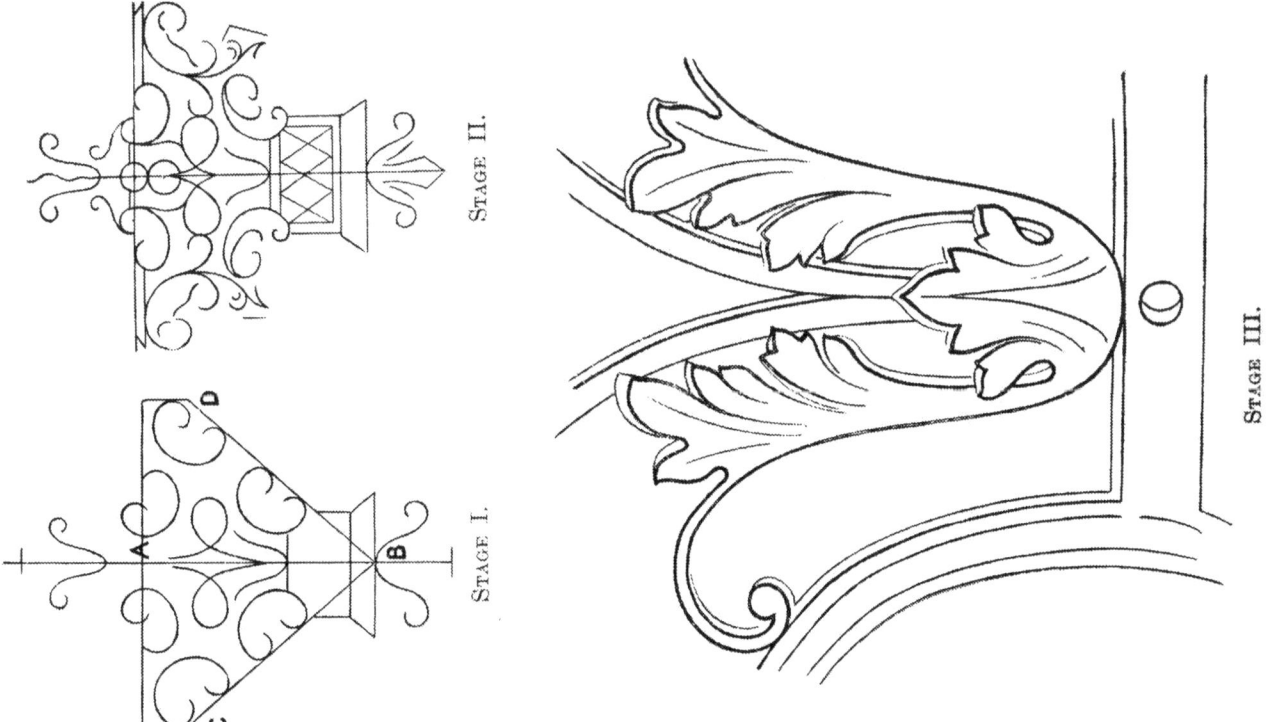

STAGE II.

STAGE I.

STAGE III.

PART OF WROUGHT IRON GATE. GERMAN (C. 1700).

By permission, South Kensington Museum

PLATE XXI.

THE LAUREL

A Spray from Nature.

STAGE I.—Set out the rectangle and then draw the leading lines, keeping them as straight as possible. This will give *vigour* which is so essential to natural foliage.

STAGE II.—Add the blocks, which enclose the masses of the leaves; also the block forms of the separate leaves. Notice how often *straight* lines are used.

STAGE III.—Read the section of the Introduction dealing with the drawing of natural foliage. Note the difference in the appearance of the mid-rib on the front of the leaf as compared with the back. The veins should be very faint and their curve made up of a series of *straight* sections. Read up particularly about the "joints" of leaves with the stems. Line in with pen or brush as shown. No wash is to be added.

PLATE XXI.

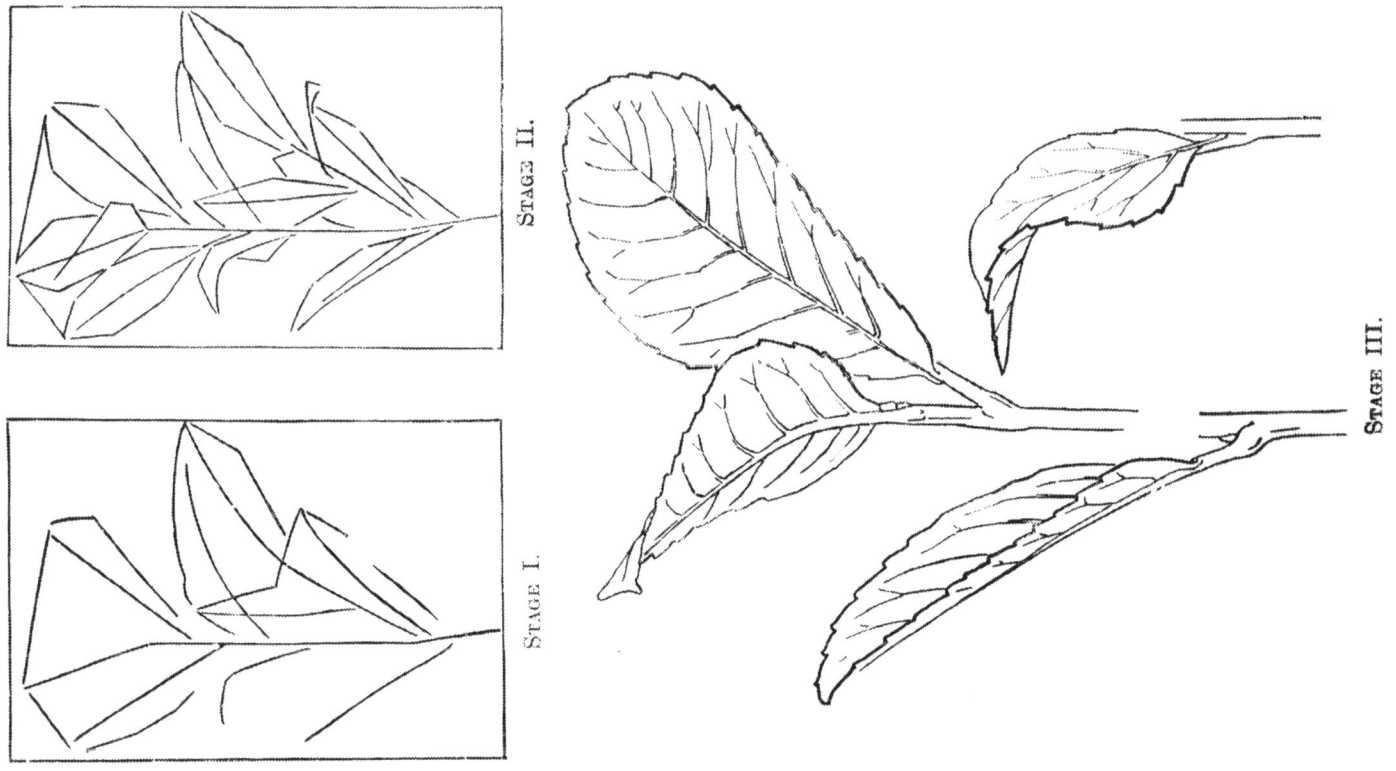

STAGE II.

STAGE I.

STAGE III.

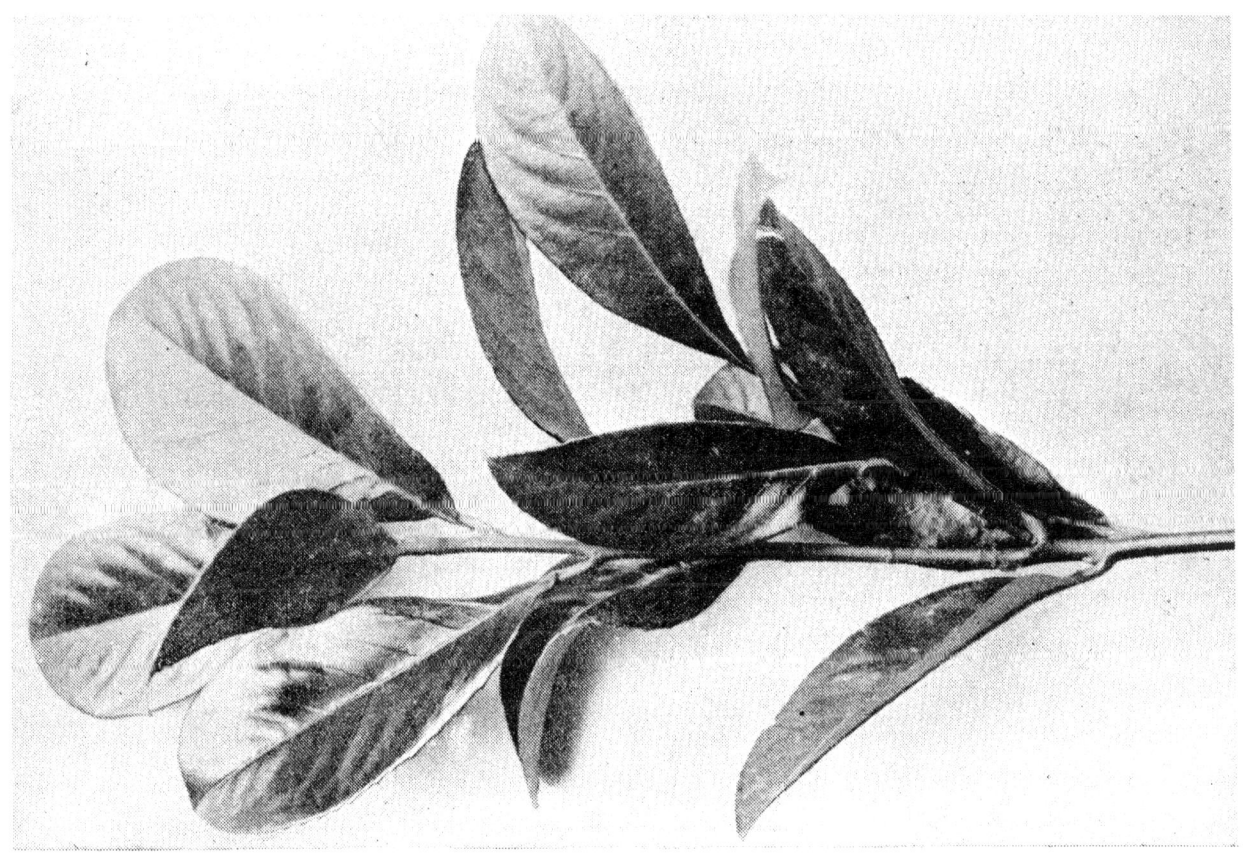

An original photograph.

LAUREL SPRAY. FROM NATURE.

PLATE XXII.

WILD ROSE

A Spray from Nature.

Stage I.—Set out the rectangle and leading lines and keep them as straight and vigorous as possible.

Stage II.—First fill in the "blocks" of the *masses* of the leaves. Next sketch the shapes of all the leaves and berries in each block.

Stage III.—Draw the stems and their details. Lastly finish a portion as shown, with pen or brush according to instruction.

N.B.—Restore parts of leaves eaten away.

PLATE XXII.

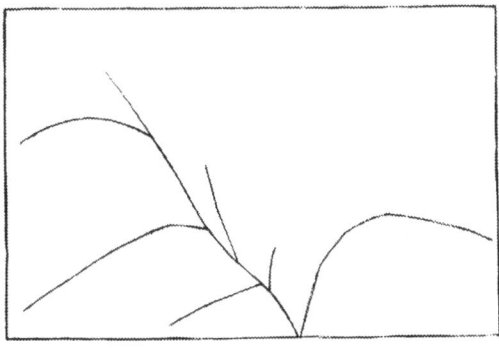

Stage I.

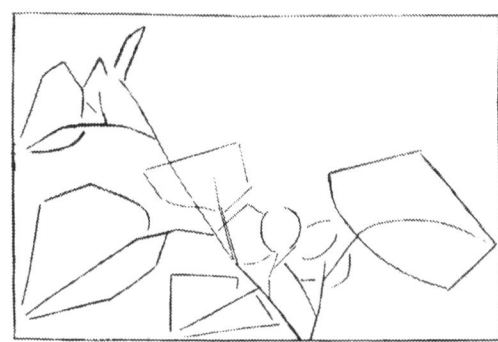

Stage II.

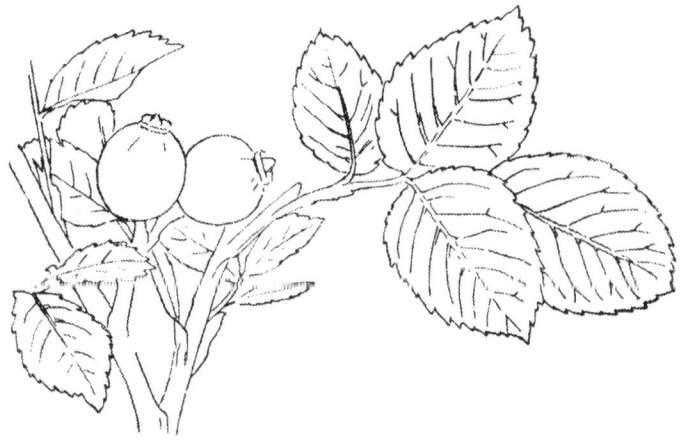

Stage III.

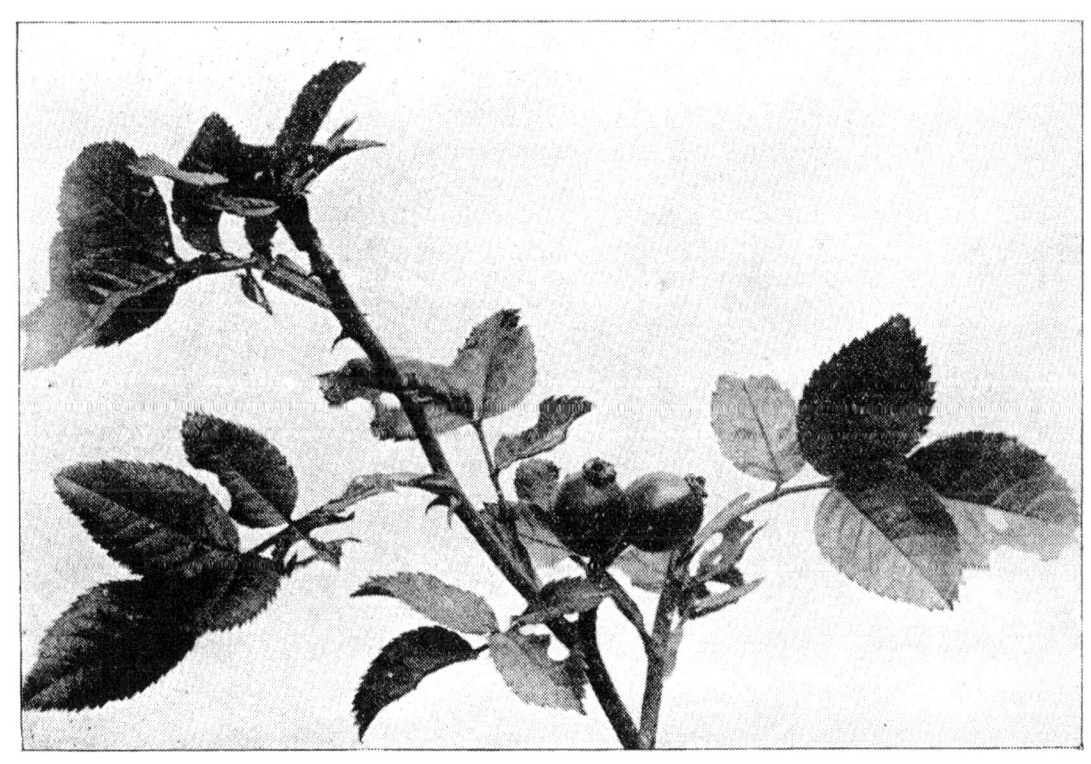

Spray of Wild Rose. From Nature.

By permission of Mr. G. B. Clough.

PLATE XXIII.

SPOT DIAPER BROCADE.

**Brocade woven in Red, Green and Yellow Silk on a Cream Silk Ground.
Italian 17th Century.**

STAGE I —Before commencing this copy read carefully through the chapter on "Construction of Pattern." Set out the required net and draw the "spot" forms (in this case horse-shoe).

STAGE II.—Into each "spot' fill in the block forms of the design.

STAGE III.—Draw *one spot* at least completely, finishing with pen or brush. A wash can be added as shown

PLATE XXIII

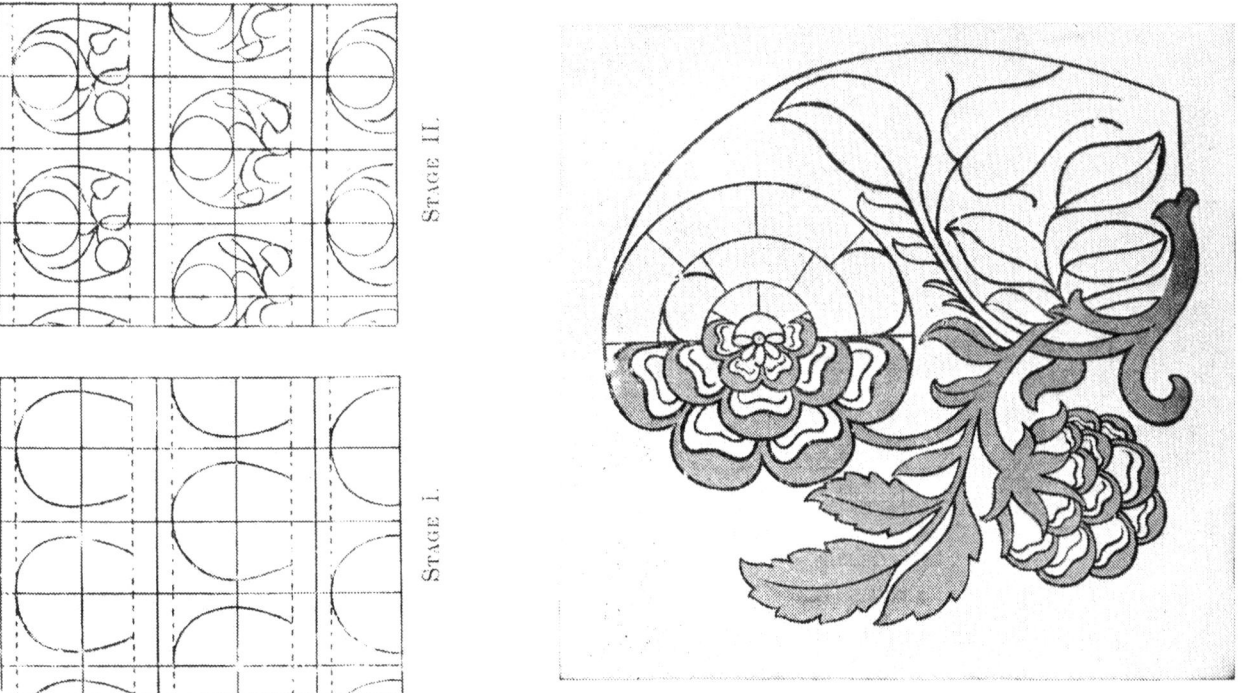

STAGE II.

STAGE I.

STAGE III.

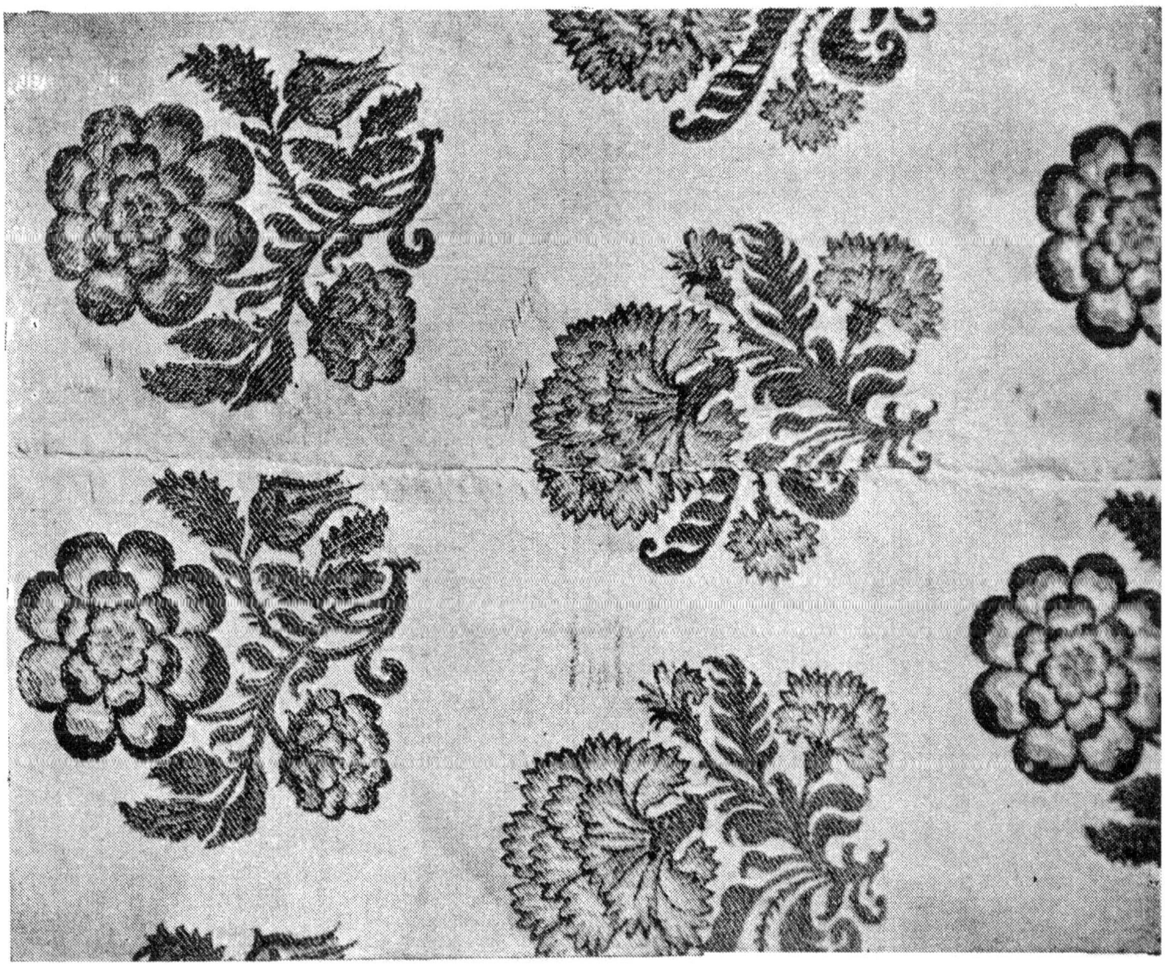

By permission, South Kensington Museum.

SPOT DIAPER BROCADE. ITALIAN 17TH CENTURY.

(61)

PLATE XXIV.

TEXTILE FABRIC.

Silk Fabric; Diaper of Fleur-de-lys and Scrolls in Gold on Crimson Ground. Italian late 16th Century.

STAGE I.—Set out the rectangle in proper proportion and then the net, and fill in the motive of circles.

STAGE II.—In each circle draw the "blocks" and also fill into them the chief forms of the fleur-de-lys.

STAGE III —Draw at least one unit of the design as shown, either in outline or in silhouette.   (See Plate XII.)

PLATE XXIV.

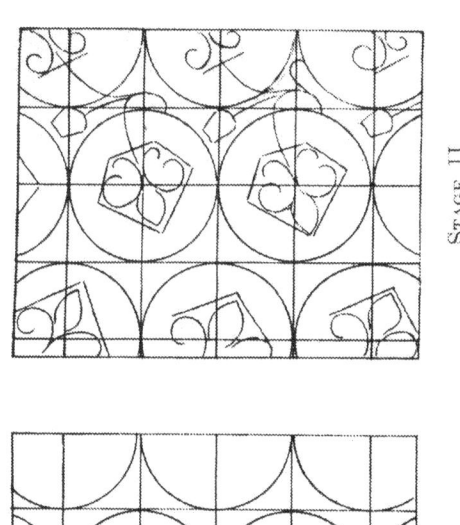

STAGE II.

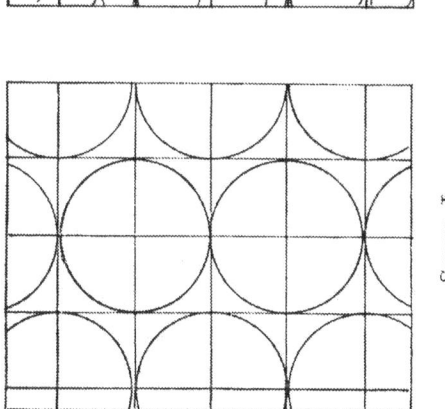

STAGE I.

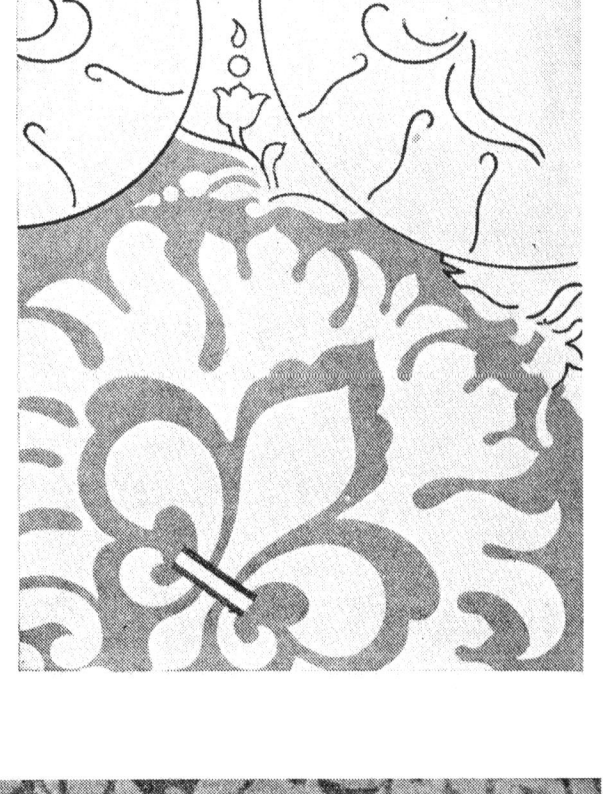

STAGE III.

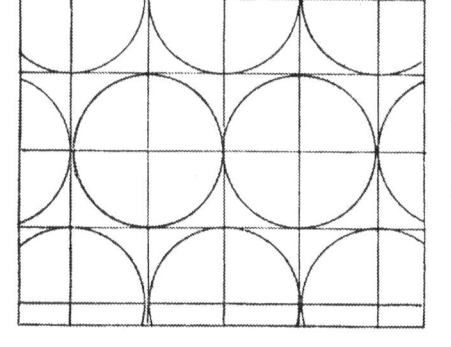

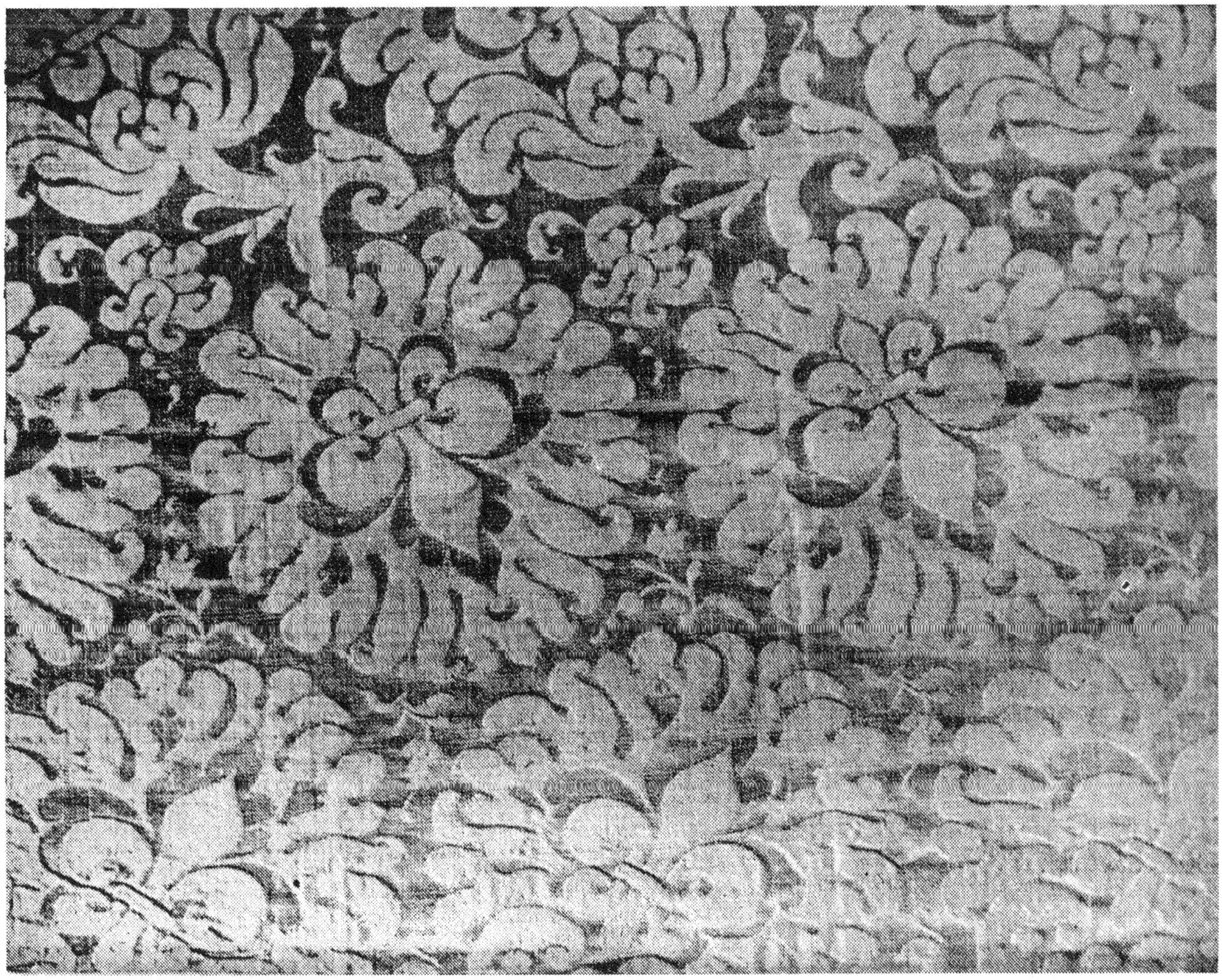

SILK FABRIC. ITALIAN LATE 16TH CENTURY.

By permission, South Kensington Museum.

PLATE XXV.

―――――

TURKISH BROCADE.

―――――

Coloured Silk and Gold Thread on a Crimson Ground in Ogees with a Border of Flowers on a Gold Ground. Turkish 17th Century. Tulips, Carnations, and Pomegranates.

―――――

STAGE I.—Draw the rectangular net as shown and sketch the "motive" of ogees. Read up the section of the Introduction dealing with Pattern Construction.

STAGE II.—Draw the borders of the ogees and add all the "block" forms in the ogees.

STAGE III. - Draw *one ogee* completely, at least. lining in with pen or brush (a small portion is shown). No wash need be added

PLATE XXV.

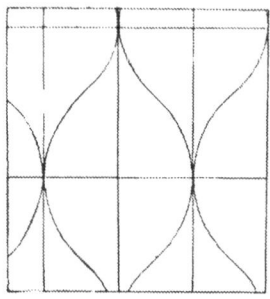

STAGE I.

STAGE II.

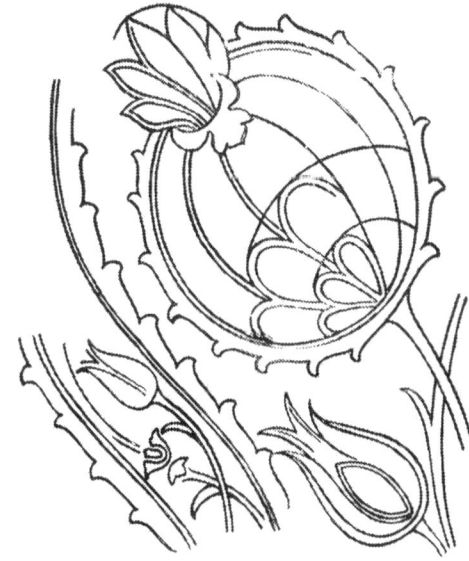

STAGE III.

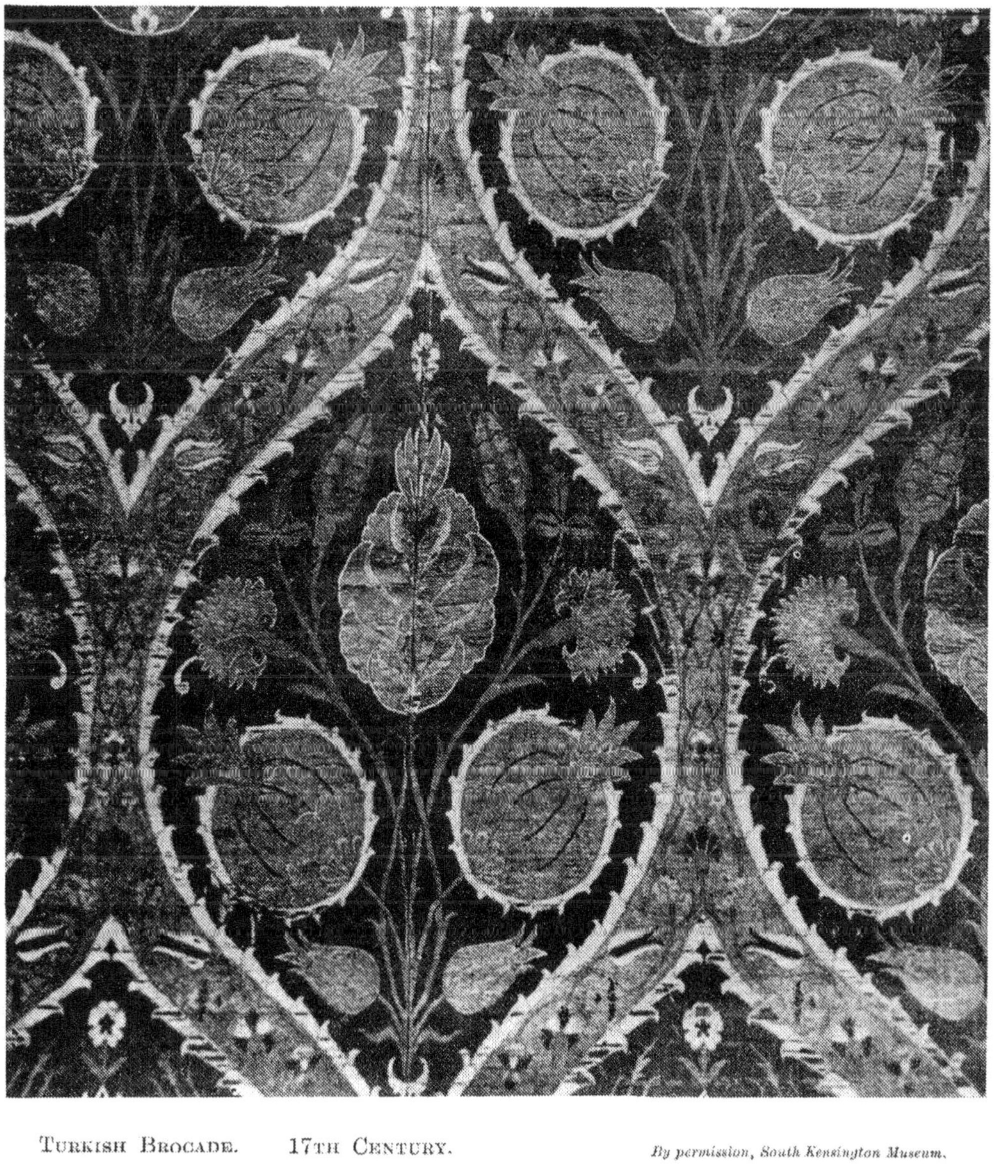

TURKISH BROCADE.   17TH CENTURY.   *By permission, South Kensington Museum.*

(65)

PLATE XXVI.

DAMASK BROCADE.

**Brocade woven in Silver Gilt Thread and Cream-coloured Silk on Cream Satin.
Italian 17th Century.**

STAGE I.—Draw the rectangular net required and add the *motive* of scale forms (Imbrication).

STAGE II —Fill in the masses of the design as shown

STAGE III.—Draw the details in *one repeat* at least as shown. The damask (the light design surrounding the dark one) need not be attempted.

PLATE XXVI.

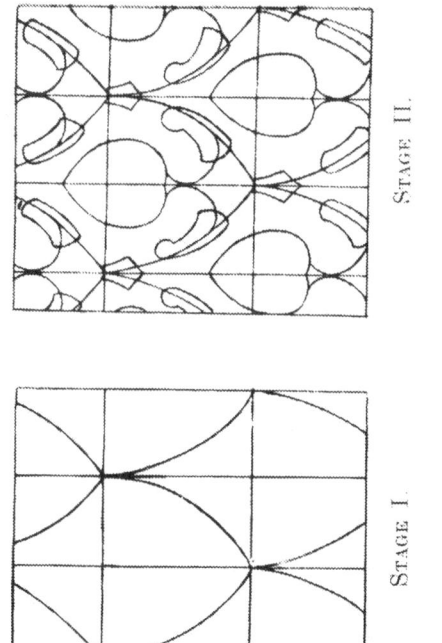

STAGE II.

STAGE I.

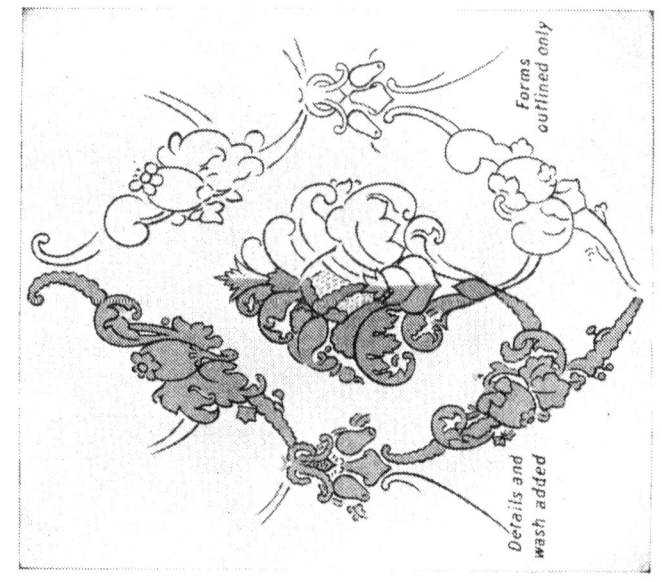

Forms
outlined only

Details and
wash added

STAGE III.

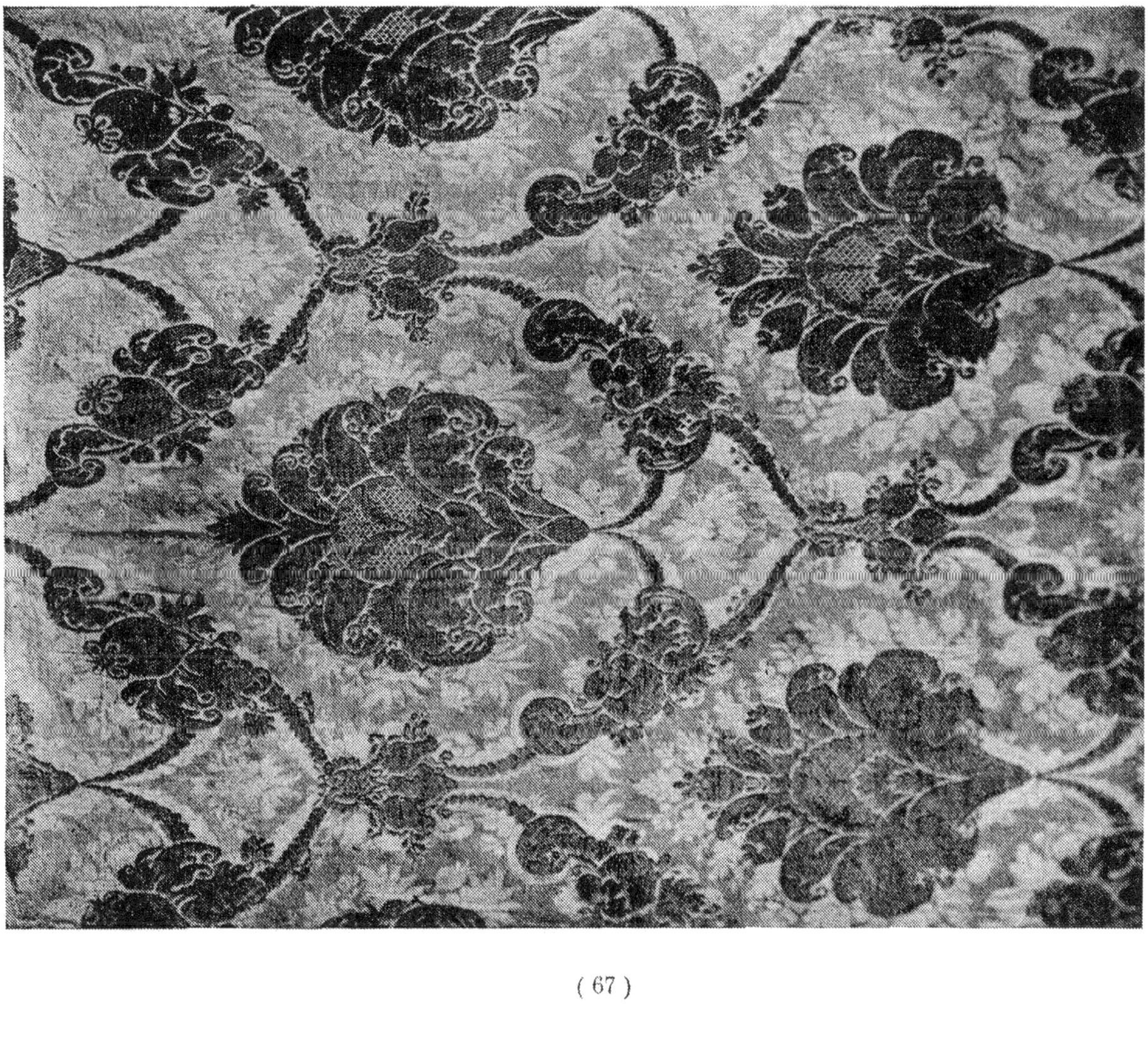

DAMASK BROCADE. ITALIAN, 17TH CENTURY.

By permission, South Kensington Museum.

PLATE XXVII,

SILK BROCADE

Turkish.   16th Century.

The Design is a wave "motive" based upon a rectangular net.

PLATE XXVII.

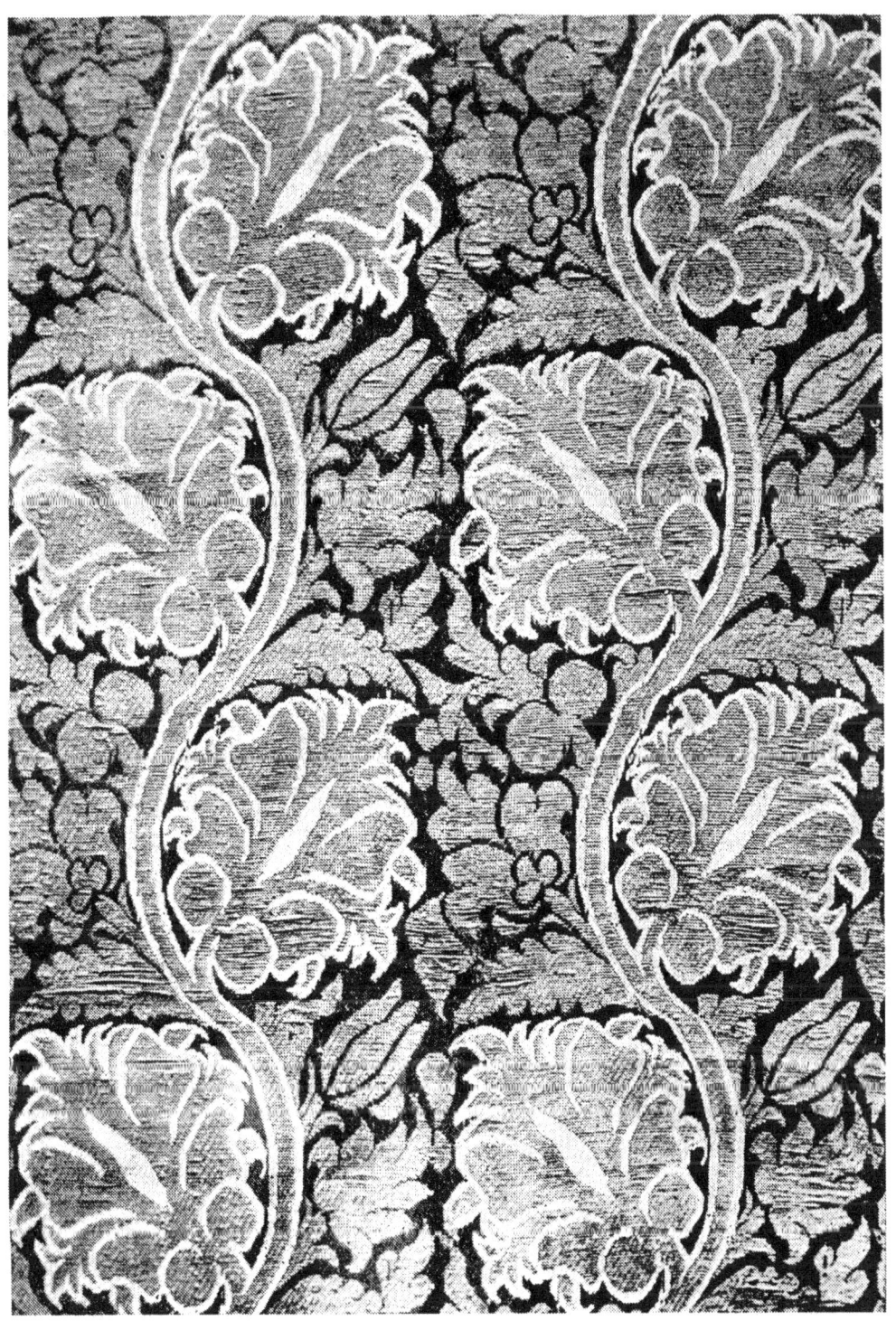

SILK BROCADE. TURKISH 16TH CENTURY.

By permission, South Kensington Museum.

PLATE XXVIII.

─────

DAMASK BROCADE.

─────

Crimson Silk Damask Ground; Design in Gold and Silver Thread. Italian, 17th Century.

─────────────

Oblique wave "motive" on a triangular net.

PLATE XXVIII.

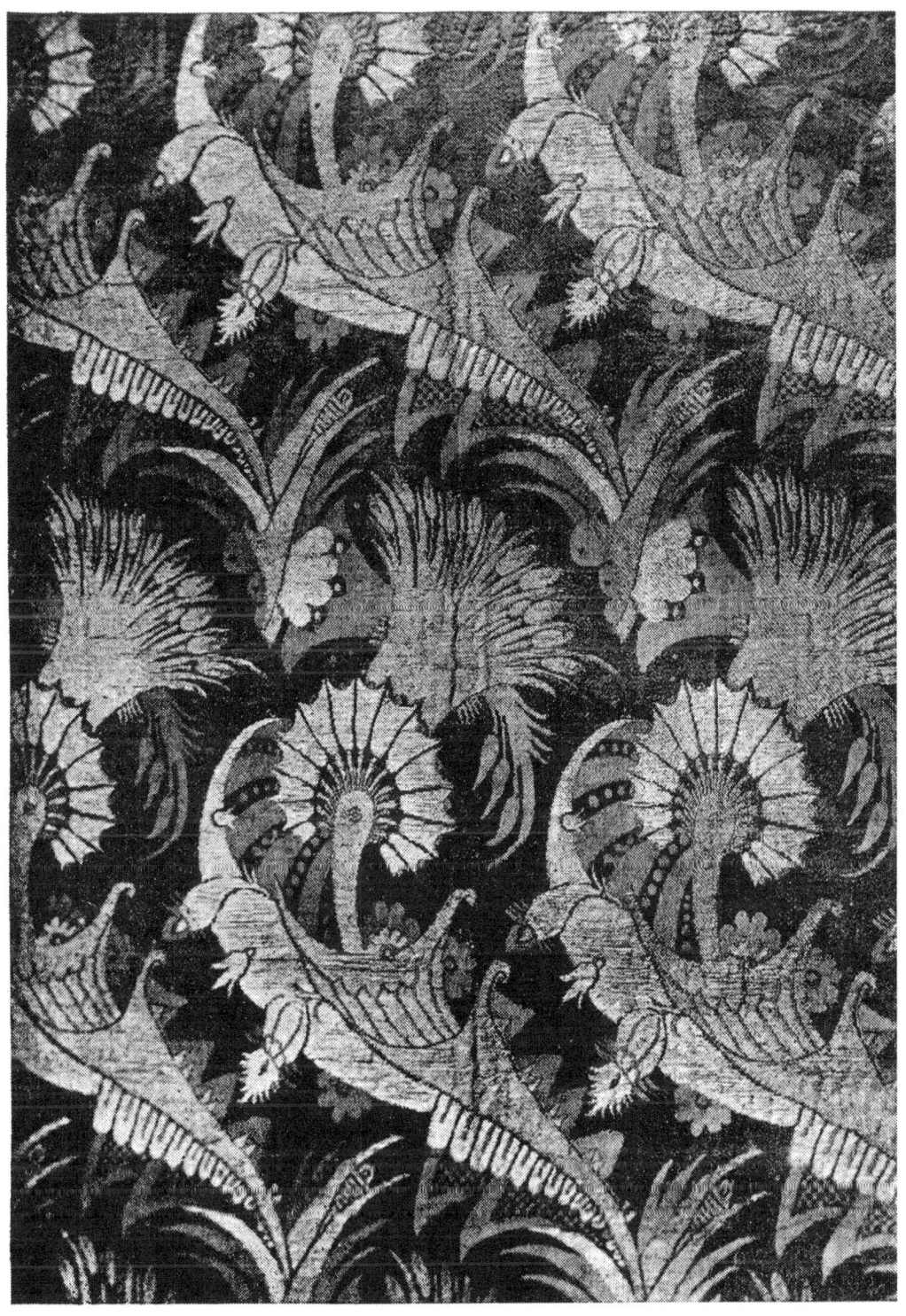

DAMASK BROCADE.   ITALIAN 17TH CENTURY.   *By permission, South Kensington Museum.*

PLATE XXIX.

THE JAPANESE ANEMONE.

A Spray from Nature: White Petals, with Green and Yellow Centre.

STAGES I. & II.—Set out the whole spray on the method described on Plate XXI., carrying it as far as the block forms for the blossoms and the leaves. Half close the eyes and look at the spray with the idea only of seeing the shapes of the masses. See that each block is of the right shape and size, and in its correct position before proceeding with the drawing of the forms.

STAGE III.—The construction for each bud and blossom is given in the diagrams. Notice that buds are built up upon the spheroid, having lines similar to those of meridians on the globe. Draw a spheroid with a number of these radiating meridians upon it, and then draw upon them the markings of the bud. The meridians will give the curves required to obtain a proper representation of the bulbous nature of the bud.

Many half opened blossoms are based upon the hemisphere, with radiating meridians upon it, somewhat similar to those of the spheroid. Make a large number of radiating lines and use those required to give the form of the petals.

In the case of an open blossom the radiating lines are almost in a plane, and the curves are therefore very slight. Draw a large number and use just those which give the forms of the petals required.

No blossom or bud should be attempted without the use of these radiating lines; they are absolutely essential to good drawing.

In the case of the leaves, first draw the mid-rib, and then the shape of the leaf itself; after that add the veins and serrations as required. Be very careful with the joining of the stalks to the stems. Read the note on this at the beginning of the book.

The near edges of blossoms and leaves should be stronger than the remote edges.

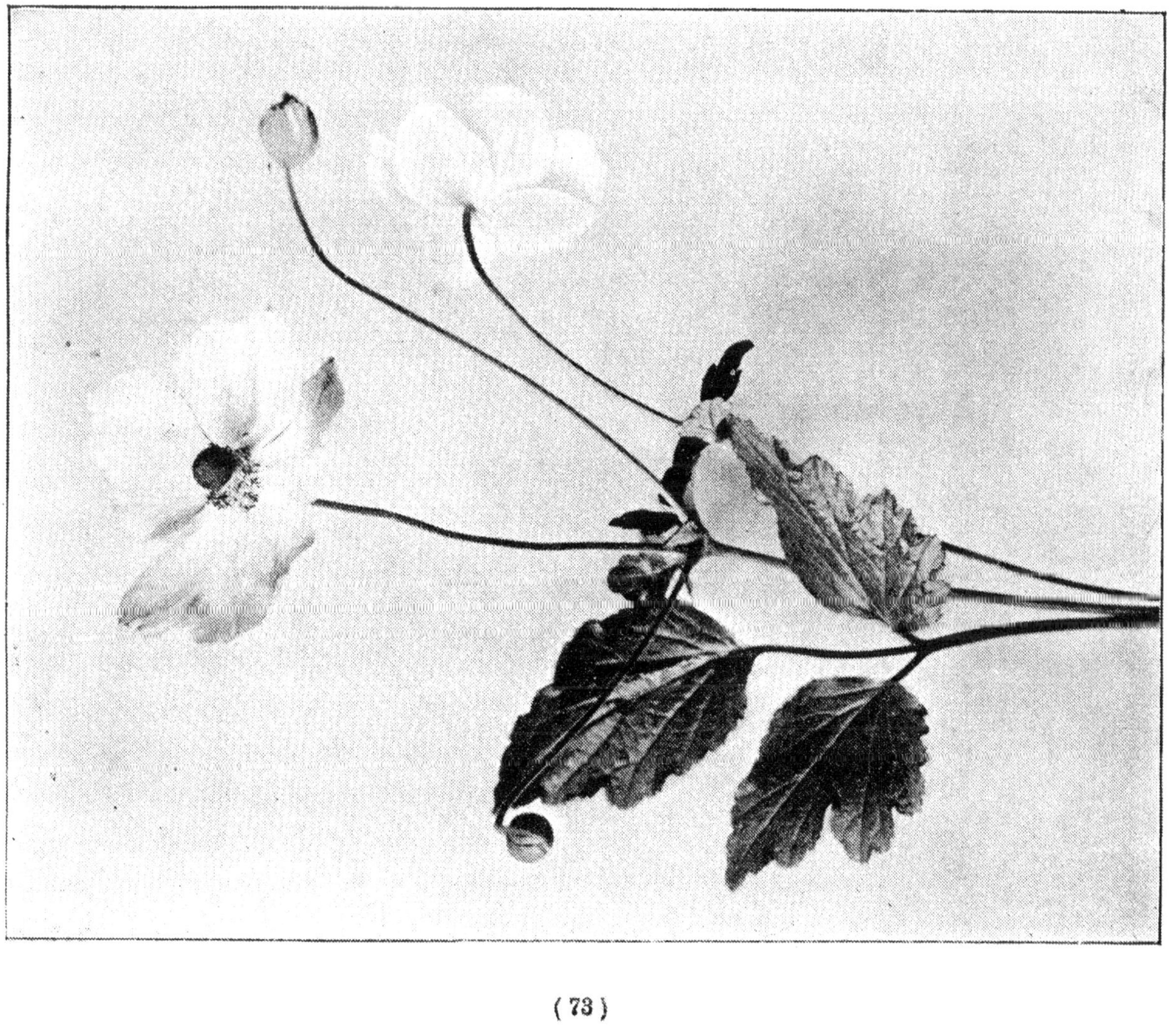

PLATE XXIX.

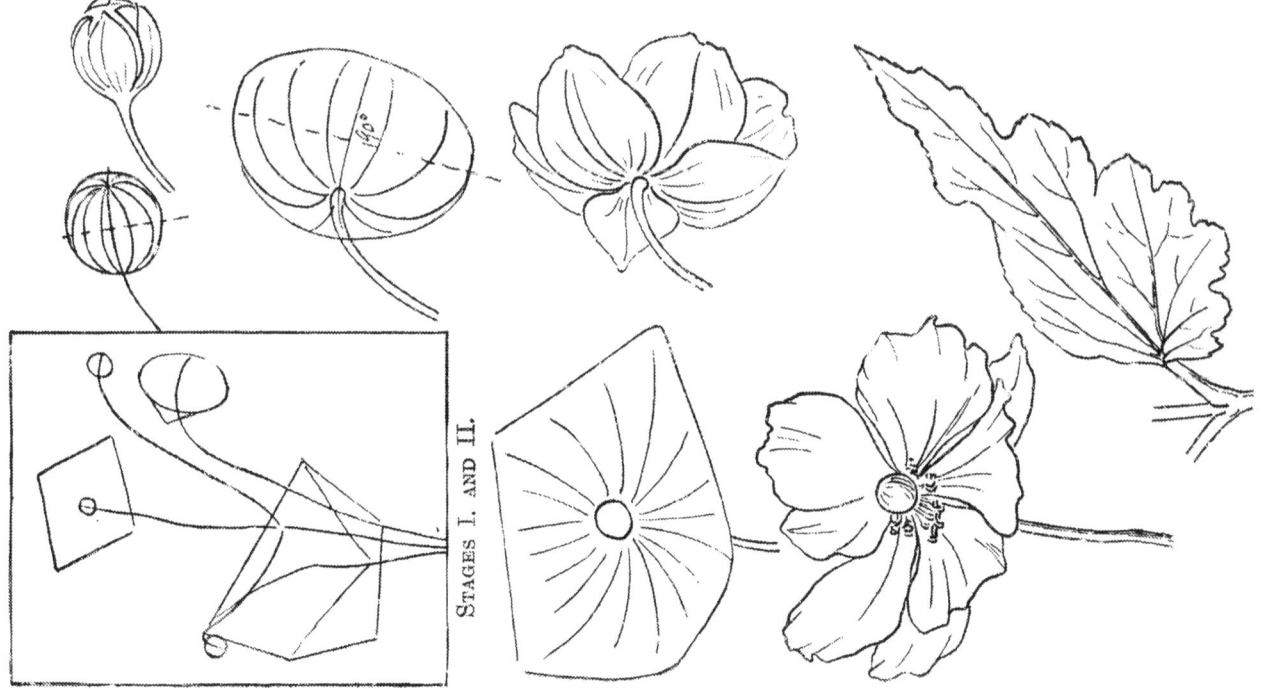

STAGES I. AND II.

JAPANESE ANEMONE. FROM NATURE.

(An Original Photograph.

PLATE XXX.

THE SCARLET GERANIUM.

A Spray from Nature.

STAGES I. & II.—Set the spray out according to previous instruction.

STAGE III.—A construction is given for the blossom. Each floweret is practically a number of petals radiating almost in a plane. Mark each centre, and then draw any number (the more the better) of radiating slightly curved lines. Upon them build up the petals and the markings on the petals. Notice that the stalks of the flowerets and buds radiate from a centre at the top of the stem. Keep the markings on the petals very faint, just as is done with veins in leaves.

A construction is also shown for the right hand leaf with radiating lines upon which to draw the veins.

The left hand leaf has been fully drawn upon the principle of the construction of the right hand leaf. Notice here the radiation of the veins. The Net veins should be made of *straight* sections lightly but sharply drawn. In all foreshortened leaves and blossoms the near edges should be drawn more strongly (*i.e.*, darkly) than those more remote. Note this in the accompanying drawings.

PLATE XXX.

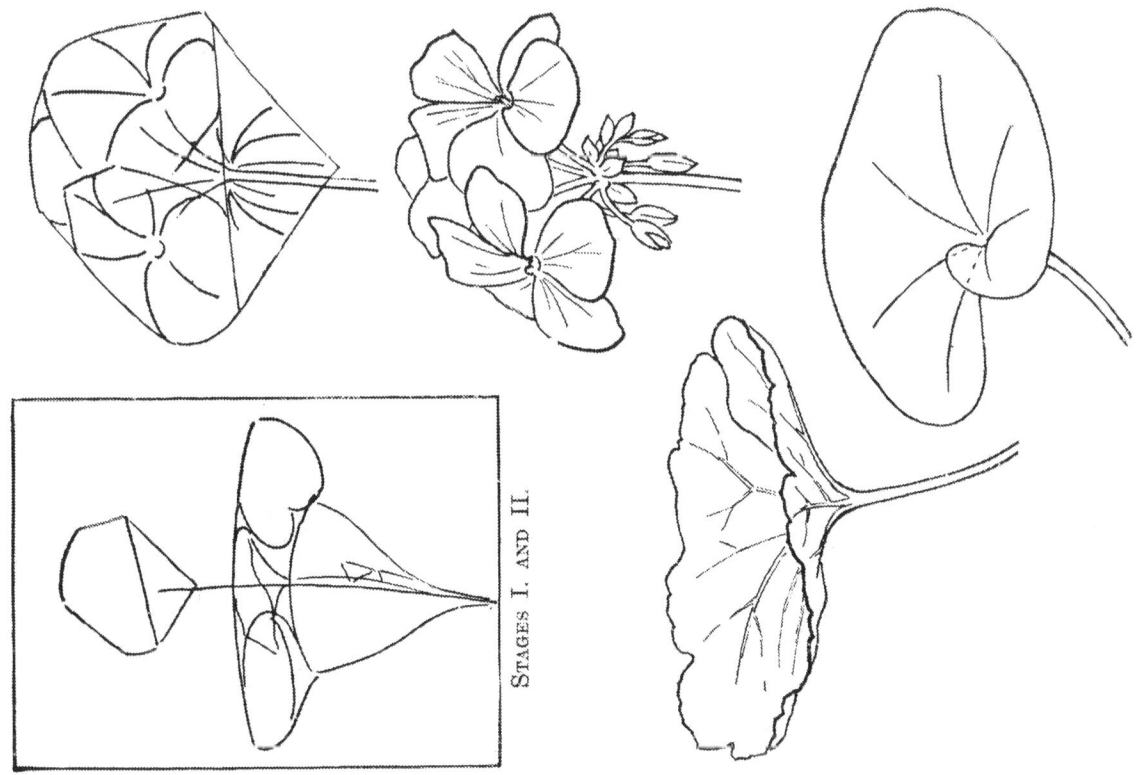

Stages I. and II.

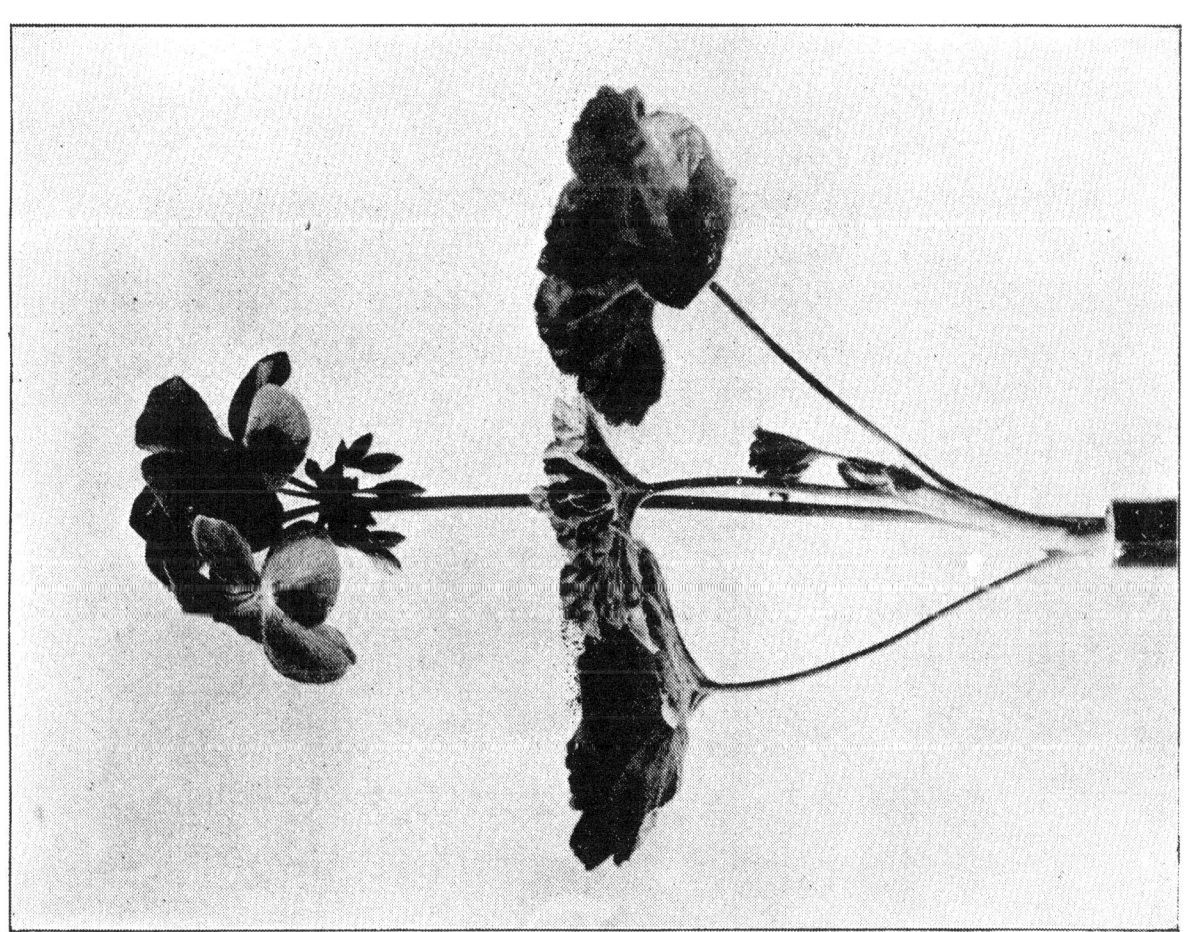

Scarlet Geranium. From Nature.

[An Original Photograph.

PLATE XXXI.

THE WHITE LILY.

A Spray from Nature.

Stages I. & II.—Set out carefully according to previous instructions.

Stage III.—A construction is shown for the blossom. It will be observed that the blossom is *cone* shaped, *i.e.*, bell or trumpet shaped. It must therefore be built up on radiating lines forming the sides of a curvilinear cone. The sides of the petals, their central vein, and other markings must all radiate from the apex of the cone.

Many flowers are based on this construction, such as the Gladiolus, Petunia, Tobacco, Convolvulus. Many others, when partly opened, are also based on the cone.

To draw the construction, make an axis and then balance an ellipse at right angle upon it, as shown. This ellipse carries the tips of the petals. It is not necessary that this ellipse should be perfect, a rough sketch is practically all that is required. Next draw a large number of radiating lines and upon them build up the petals.

The leaves of this plant are simple. A little care is required with the fore-shortened view.

First draw the mid-rib (*i.e.*, central vein) and then the two edges complete, whether seen or not.

The node or place of attachment requires careful treatment. Read up Page 10.

The secondary veins on the leaves should be very lightly drawn, and should *radiate.*

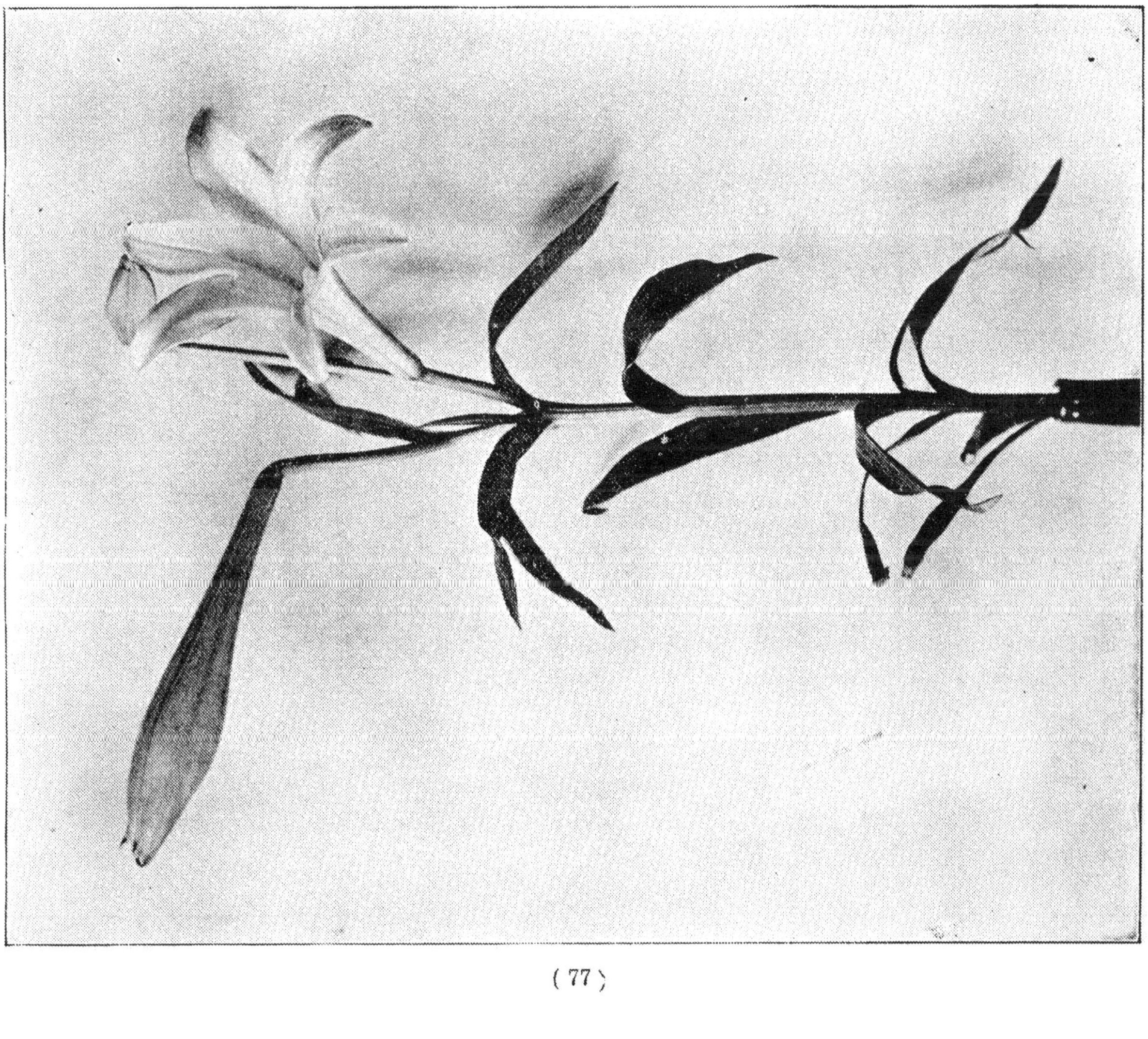

PLATE XXXI.

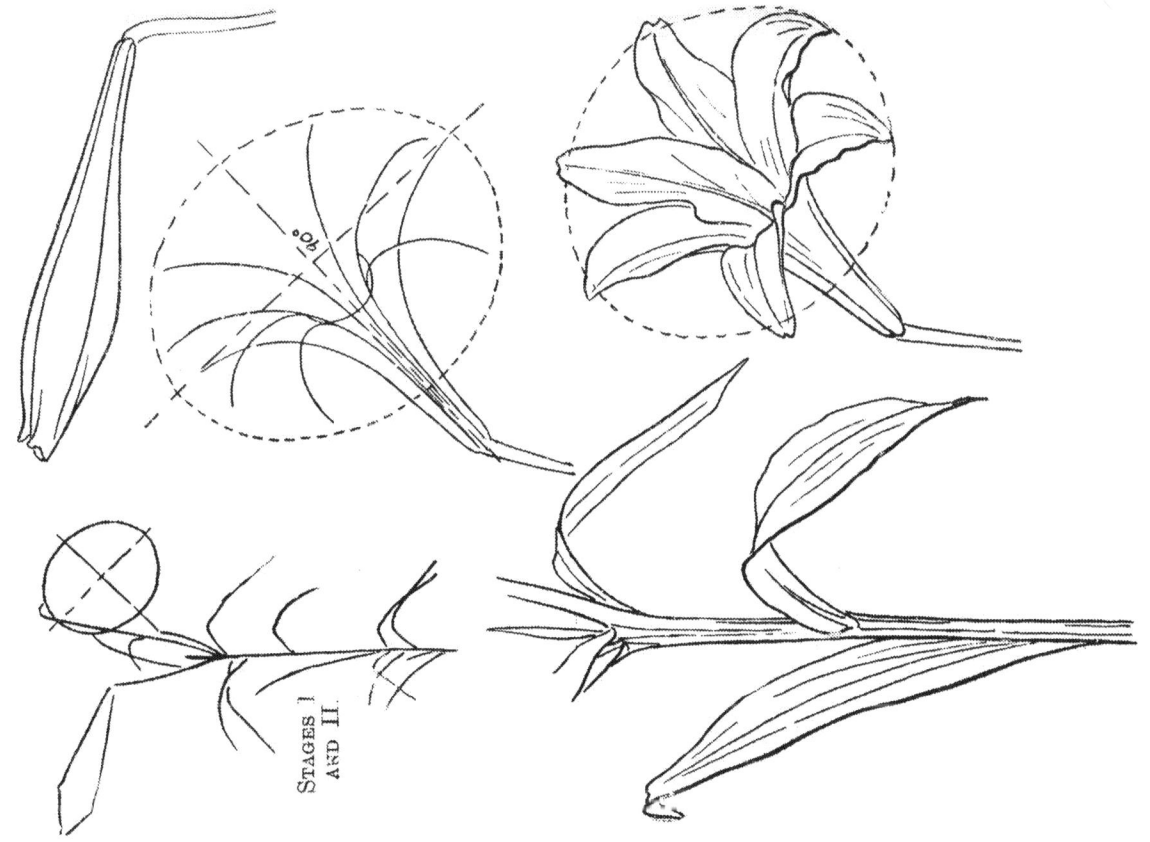

STAGES I AND II.

WHITE LILY. FROM NATURE.

[An Original Photograph.

PLATE XXXII.

THE GLADIOLUS.

A Spray from Nature.

STAGES I. & II.—Set the spray out according to previous instructions.

STAGE III.—A construction is shown for the drawing of the floweret, which is based upon the cone, just as in the case of the White Lily. Draw an ellipse to take the tips of the petals, and then put in a *large* number of radiating lines (more than those shown in the drawing) upon the curved sides of the cone. Base the petals and their markings upon the radiating lines. The leaves are extremely simple. The veining consists of long radiating lines.

PLATE XXXII

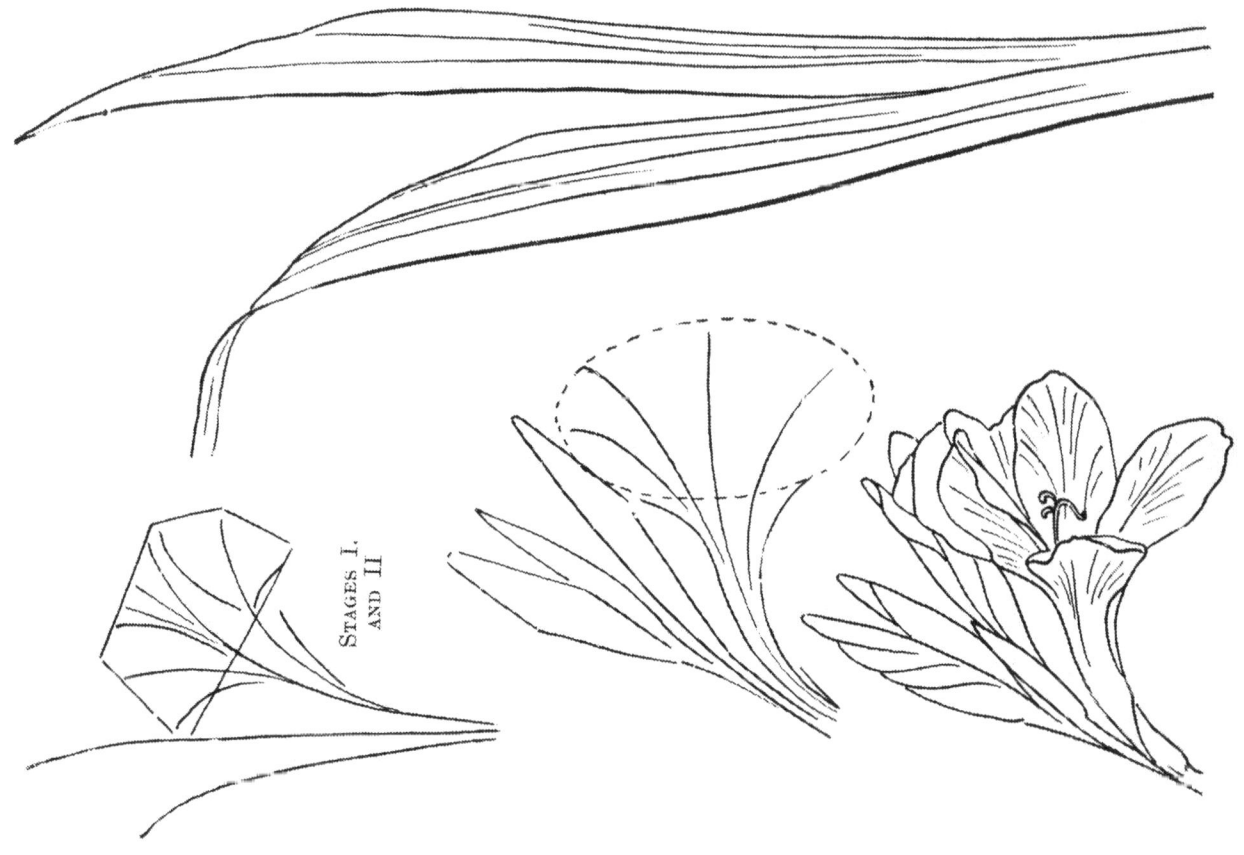

STAGES I. AND II

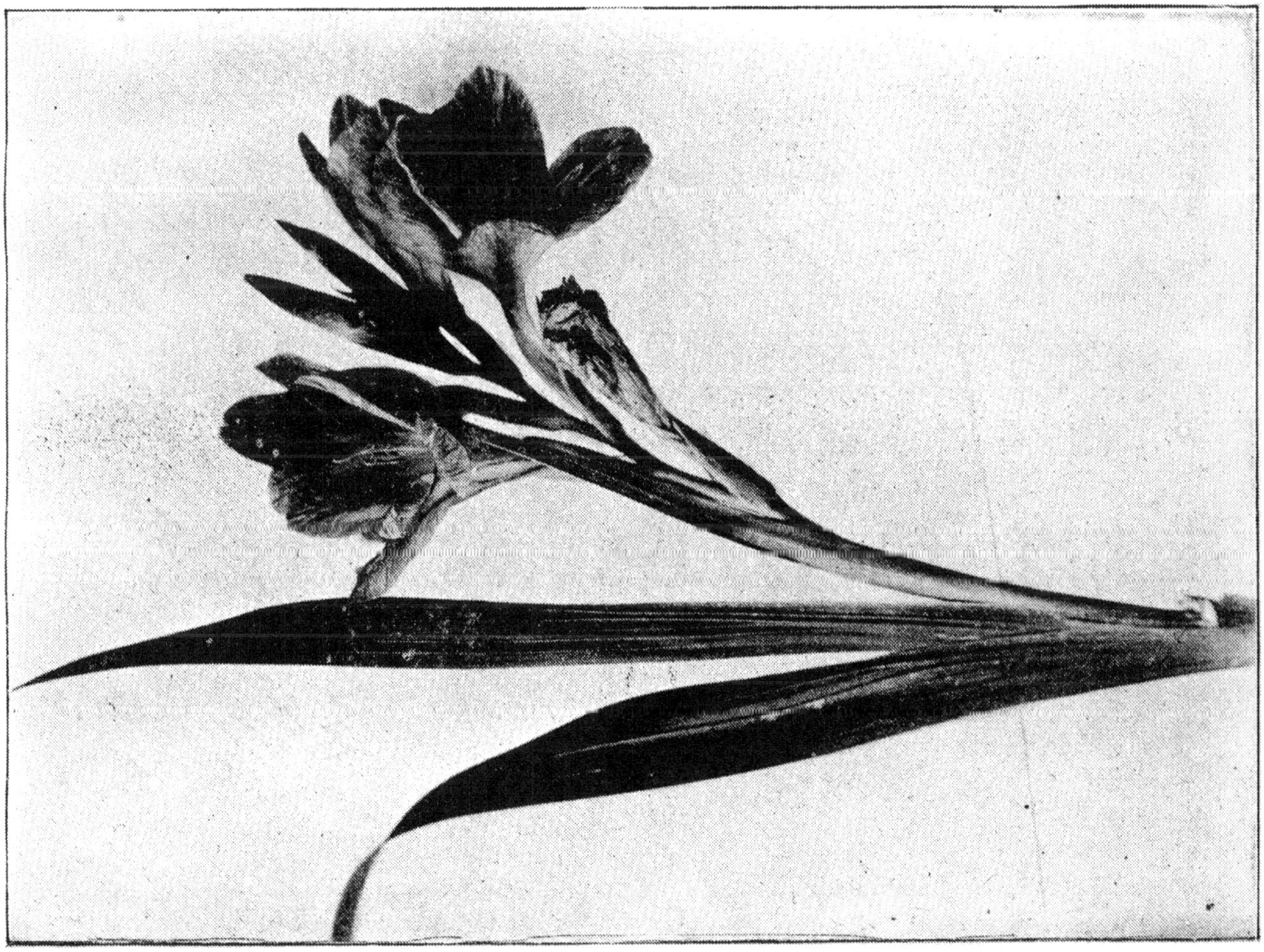

GLADIOLUS. FROM NATURE.

www.ingramcontent.com/pod-product-compliance
Lightning Source LLC
Chambersburg PA
CBHW081726220526
45468CB00008B/1996